The

THE MADCHESTER SCENE

www.pocketessentials.com

First published in Great Britain 2002 by Pocket Essentials, 18 Coleswood Road, Harpenden, Herts, AL5 1EQ

Distributed in the USA by Trafalgar Square Publishing, PO Box 257, Howe Hill Road, North Pomfret, Vermont 05053

Copyright © Richard Luck 2002
Series Editor: Paul Duncan

A CIP catalogue record for this book is available from the British Library.

ISBN 1-903047-80-3

2 4 6 8 10 9 7 5 3 1

Book typeset by Pdunk
Printed and bound by Cox & Wyman

To Harry, for making the Luck family happier than it ever thought it could be.

This book is dedicated to the memory of Rob Gretton.

"I met Rob in town one day and he asked if he could manage us. I said: 'yes, come down to rehearsals next Monday,' but unfortunately I forgot to tell the rest of the group. So Rob turned up and everyone just turned round and said: 'who's this grey-haired, beer-swilling polar bear?' So I said: 'Forgot to tell you, forgot to tell you - he's our new manager. How about it?' So we gave him a trial and he turned out to be... very adequate."

- Bernard Sumner, Joy Division/New Order

Acknowledgements

Many, many thanks to: my sister-in-law Emma who somehow balanced subbing and research duties with the ordeals that are raising a young child and being married to my brother; to Matt Jeary for web surfing above and beyond the call of duty; to Dan Jolin, my reviews editor at *Total Film*, for giving me the inside rub on *24 Hour Party People*; to Al Spicer, Mark Ellingham and Jonathan Buckley for breaking me in as a music writer; to Paul Duncan and Ion Mills for so many reasons; and to John Ashbrook for the greatest gift a friend can give - a career.

CONTENTS

1. Wrote For Luck 7

A preface by the author

2. Madchester - So Much To Answer For 9

An introduction to the scene with snapshots of some of its personalities

3. Forefathers 26

Buzzcocks, Joy Division, New Order, The Fall, The Smiths

4. The Big Two 43

The Stone Roses, Happy Mondays

5. The Also-Bands 61

The Charlatans, James, Inspiral Carpets, 808 State, Primal Scream, Electronic, Oasis

6. Lost In Music 80

The bands that didn't make it: Northside, The Mock Turtles, Flowered Up, The High

7. Bog Awful Baggy 82

Bands that just didn't get it: EMF, The Farm, Jesus Jones, Blur, The Soup Dragons, Candy Flip

8. Rave On? 85

Madchester lives on in the film 24 Hour Party People

9. Reference Materials 91

Books, videos, DVDs and Websites

1. Wrote For Luck

"I've finally got a group," exclaimed the then 26-year-old Ewan McGregor to *Neon* magazine in 1997 on having fallen in love with Oasis. It took me a long time to find a band, too - not as freakishly long as Ewan but a long time, nonetheless. I'd been buying records for years (pretty haphazardly, mind you. I'm sure I was one of the few 13-year-olds to own records by both Grandmaster Flash and Bucks Fizz), but while I'd bought copies of 'Shellshock' and 'State Of The Nation,' it wasn't until the release of the New Order compilation *Substance* and the single 'True Faith' that I truly found my sound.

I can't really put my finger on the appeal of New Order and perhaps that's how it should be. But I can say that I liked the story behind the band. I was impressed by their earlier work as Joy Division. I respected them for what they'd gone through. I loved the sublime swash of their synthesisers and admired the fact that a skinny rabbit like Steven Morris could land a place in a pop group. I liked the fact that Bernard Sumner sung in a voice so fragile it couldn't disguise his sincerity and I was choked by the fact that here was a band who told you how it is and then showed you how wonderful it could be. But what special ingredient X made me feel for them in ways I'd never felt about any other band, I couldn't say and I couldn't care. Within a month of buying *Substance*, I owned the entire New Order/Joy Division album back catalogue.

And from there, I became a follower of most things Madchester. I picked up The Stone Roses' 'Elephant Stone' because it was produced by Peter Hook and then bought their debut album during the first week of release. I bought *Academy*, New Order's awful concert video which came with a T-shirt so tight, even Posh Spice would have struggled to get into it. I was even one of those fresh-faced saps who wandered into Our Price and said: "Hello, have you got *Bummed* by the Happy Mondays?"

There were, I should point out, limits to my dedication. I never grew my hair long and the only hooded top I owned was the one I trained for rugby in. But my first gig couldn't have featured a more Mancunian line-up (New Order supported by Happy Mondays) and I did pay a visit to the sainted city, although since I was on a rugby tour I was more concerned about my hamstring and my coach's experimental decision to play me out of position than about visiting the Hacienda or experimenting with E.

Of course, I could have been a more committed member of the Mad-chester community. I could have bought more records, worn more appropriate clothes, taken any drugs. But 1990, the year the movement really hit its straps, was a ludicrously happy time for me - England's glorious failure in the World Cup, visiting America and Paris, getting my rugby colours, passing A-Levels I expected to fail - and it's because this music was the soundtrack to such a great summer that I remember it so fondly and have longed to write about it so badly.

Almost a decade on, my music tastes have changed. Now I listen to Blur, Air, Rage Against The Machine, Foo Fighters, Beastie Boys, De La Soul, DJ Shadow and Daft Punk. But despite all the years that have passed and all the records I've bought, the final revelation of The Stone Roses' 'Sally Cinnamon' still chokes me up a bit, The Charlatans' 'The Only One I Know' remains one of the few songs guaranteed to bring a smile to my face, Black Grape's recapturing of the Mondays' glory couldn't have felt sweeter and I am happier than anyone that New Order never properly split up. And when The Stone Roses' 'Fools Gold' came on the sound system at LA2 on Charing Cross Road in the early hours of 1 September 2001, do you think I was there dancing like a primate with the rest of the throng? Well of course I wasn't! I'm 29 for fuck's sake! I did feel pretty privileged that I was writing a book about them, mind you.

Richard Luck
Welwyn Garden City, September 2001

2. Madchester - So Much To Answer For

"Madchester - what a name!
Best name ever for a scene, wasn't it?"

- Clint Boon, Inspiral Carpets

'And on the eighth day, God created Madchester.' That was a T-shirt slogan you saw quite a lot of in the late 1980s and early 1990s. (Tops were also available which claimed that the miracle occurred on the Lord's sixth or seventh day at the office.) It wasn't the only weird thing appearing on leisurewear around that time. You could also buy gear sporting the bland-est of monikers, Joe Bloggs, or carrying obscure out-of-context phrases like 'Come Hone.' Or, if you preferred, you could purchase a T-shirt bar-ing an image of a mashed-up cow smoking a spliff and the legend 'Cool As Fuck.'

The one thing you didn't see a lot of back then were shirts bearing the crests of Manchester City or Manchester United. Utterly dominant in recent years, it's incredible to think that Man U were really on the ropes at the ass end of the 1980s. Outside of a few FA Cup wins, the team had achieved little during the decade outside of sacking managers, fielding players who weren't up to the task (Mike Duxbury, anyone?) and getting ever so frightfully pissed off about finishing second to Liverpool. As for the men from Maine Road, meanwhile, their parlous state was best summed up by Steve Coogan's pissed-up, pissed-off scrounger Paul Calf: "I had a trial for Man City but I was terrible - missed an open goal, headed it into my own net, I was absolutely shite. Anyway, they offered me a place... but I was sixteen - I wanted to concentrate on smoking. But you can say what you like about Manchester City. You can say they've gone down, you can say they're rubbish, you can say they're the biggest shower of shite you've ever seen but... I forget the original point I was making."

As soccer was always seen as being the heartbeat of Manchester, you'd imagine this sort of failure might have caused a metropolis-sized depres-sion. But it didn't and the reason it didn't was the most exciting musical movement since the Two-Tone explosion of a decade earlier: Madchester.

But what was Madchester? Well, like a lot of youth movements, Mad-chester was about being young, dumb and full of come. But it was about so many other things. Yes, it was about being naïve, but it was also about knowing yourself. It was about having a bit of money, a plectrum and a few grams of your 'medicine' of choice in your pocket. It was about drinking beer but also quaffing litre after litre of water. It was about altering Manchester street signs so that they now carried the name of the scene. It was about experimenting with E, blagging bennies and coke, and maybe even rediscovering glue. It was about eating stodge just to soak up the booze and pick up the 'poison.' It was about talking in an exaggerated Mancunian accent whether you came from Hulme or Hythe. It was about using words and phrases like 'bangin',' 'sorted,' 'crackin',' 'top one,' 'kickin',' 'blindin'' and 'on one.' It was about growing your hair really long and then cutting it with the aid of a bowl. It was about buggering up your posture, hunching up your shoulders, scuffing your feet on the floor when you walked and swinging your arms like you were Galen from *Planet Of The Apes*. It was about dancing like a monkey. It was about staying out so late, you got up before you fell asleep. It was about constantly looking as if you were in need of a few hours kip and a gallon of orange juice. It was about romanticising gang culture and graffiti even though you probably weren't in a gang and almost certainly didn't own an aerosol. It was about hanging outside warehouses on the off chance that there was something going down inside and thinking that it would be great to be a drug dealer even though you were probably going to wind up working in a bank. What's more, it was about owning albums such as Happy Mondays' *Bummed* and *Pills 'N' Thrills & Bellyaches*, Inspiral Carpets' *Life*, James' *Gold Mother* and The Stone Roses' er... *The Stone Roses*. It was about referring to yourself as a 'scally' irrespective of the term's negative connotations. It was about pouring a pint of lager over your head at the Hacienda i) to help you cool down and ii) because you felt like it. It was about wearing outsized T-shirts, huge hooded tops and bog-awful beanie hats. It was about sporting labels like Reebok, Kangol and Joe Bloggs. It was about wearing a pair of jeans with 19 inch bottoms that threatened to trip you up every time you took a step. It was about learning to like a city in spite of its shite weather, hideous 1960s architecture and absence of certainties. It was about realising that no matter how shit things got, there was another great Saturday night just around the corner. It was about realising how terrifying life was and then choosing not to be afraid. And it was about realising the whole world was against you and then saying: "OK, let's have it!"

So when did this party begin? Opinion is divided although people certainly agree that the North was well and truly at its heights when Spike Island, a massive concert, was staged in Widnes. It was headlined by The Stone Roses and proved that the scene could support a gig that rivalled Knebworth for size if not organisation, situation and sound quality. There's also little argument about when the scene hit the mainstream. Jackie Brambles and Jenni Powell were the hosts who brought you that 29 November 1989 edition of *Top Of The Pops*. The line-up that evening featured two Manchester acts, Happy Mondays and The Stone Roses. To be fair, the performances they gave that night were pretty lacklustre. Shaun Ryder struggled to remember the lyrics to 'Hallelujah' that he was supposed to lip-synch to, Ian Brown looked like he couldn't be bothered as he performed his simian shuffle to 'Fools Gold'; shit, if it hadn't been for the immaculate Kirsty McColl who guested with the Mondays that night, you could easily have overlooked either band. Mondays' dancer/vibe merchant Bez knew exactly why the groups appeared so ambivalent: "The thing about *Top Of The Pops* is that it's the most boring, crap day you've ever had. It looks great on television but in reality you're just stuck in a room with a mirror, a sink, a chair and yourselves for company." *Top Of The Pops* producer Chris Cowey, though, thought the bands were both brilliant: "It was just a complete breath of fresh air. You could feel the brooding resentment, bollocks-to-the-lot-of-you attitude coming right down the camera." Regardless of whether The Roses and Mondays were brilliant or bloody awful, by the time the show went off air, the whole country had heard of Madchester.

And as for what happened next, well, it was really quite beautiful. A small but gifted band of bands sprung up across the North-West like Oldham's Inspiral Carpets, the idiosyncratic James, the synthesiser and sample driven 808 State. You couldn't ignore them and you couldn't deny they were talented. And then groups in other parts of the country like The Charlatans from Wolverhampton and London/Glasgow's Primal Scream started to make music along similar lines, turning a local scene into a national phenomenon. Hip comedians like Rob Newman and David Baddiel made maligning Manchester a key part of their act (as well as Newman claiming that Myra Hindley should have been given a few more weeks freedom so she could have seen to James' Tim Booth and The Charlatans' Tim Burgess, the pair donned Mondays' mufti so that Newman's Ryder could ask Baddiel's Bez exactly what it was he paid him to do). Scally fashions started to be worn in places as far afield as Sittingbourne, Scarborough and Stirling. The city became the place to go to university. As critic and author John Robb explained: "If you're 18 with three A-levels, where do you want to go? Do you want to go to York because it's got lots of beautiful old buildings, or do you want to go to a city where you can party like mad? You want to go to the party city. Unless you're stupid." People began to flock to Manchester like it was an exotic holiday destination. TV presenter Gail Porter: "I went to Manchester for a weekend and stayed for three months." They talked about the Hacienda nightclub in awed tones. They made a big deal about Dry, the bar owned by New Order. They did the pills. They enjoyed the thrills. They put up with the bellyaches. They partied. Hard. "The thing about the 1960s," Robb continues, "was that there were two people in London having a party and everyone else was trying to find it. But I think Manchester was the opposite - you had 200,000 people having a party and anyone could find it."

The beat Madchester grooved to had three basic components. The first of these was funk, but we're not talking about that nice, smooth American funk that came out of Philadelphia during the 1970s. We're not even talking about the crazy-ass, aliens-in-the-ghetto, drug-induced P-funk that George Clinton made so popular. Madchester funk was an altogether scuzzier, more fucked-up affair. Raw, libidinous, deep down and dirty, it was a sound you couldn't resist but you felt like you ought to have a shower the moment you stopped listening to it.

Madchester was also characterised by a distinctive guitar sound. It had its origins in the 1960s but it was hard to trace the evolutionary path as this, too, had been dirtied up. Yes, there was a trace of the Merseybeat jangle, an element of The Kinks, a bit of The Byrds, a sniff of the Small Faces and you couldn't help but identify elements of Johnny Marr but, again, Madchester's artists had taken something invented elsewhere and put such a heavy, heady spin on it, that it now belonged to them.

Since so much emphasis was placed on accentuating the rawness of the music, someone or something was needed to add a sheen to the Madchester sound to enable it to cross over into the mainstream. The men for the job turned out to be not producers but DJs. Prior to the scene starting up, you tended to associate the term DJ with entities like Radio One. With the arrival of 808 State, who were basically a bunch of DJs who experimented with keyboards, and Factory Records' decision to let club kings Steve

Osborne and Paul Oakenfold remix the Mondays' *Pills 'N' Thrills*... not only did the Madchester sound acquire a slightly cleaner, more commercial edge but the foundations had been laid for the DJ culture that was to engulf Britain towards the end of the 1990s.

Of course, it wasn't quite that straightforward. There were other influences like the attitudes of punk and the dance sounds coming out of Ibiza, New York and Detroit. It's also worth noting that baggy bands weren't just looking overseas or to the distant past for inspiration. Indeed, Happy Monday Shaun Ryder had clearly been checking out contemporary British acts like Big Audio Dynamite, whose blend of reggae beats, hip hop breaks, alternative guitar and film dialogue samples came on like a more polished version of the Mondays' early recordings. The precision work of DJs is of special interest, however, since it was a little at odds with the general Madchester ethos. Not being able to play your instruments had been a prerequisite of being a musician in Manchester ever since the 1970s. Indeed, one of the reasons New Order hired Gillian Gilbert in 1980 was because she wasn't particularly skilled, just like the three incumbent members of the group. By the time Madchester was in full swing, the 'have guitar, can't play' ethos had reached ridiculous levels. That a man like Mark 'Bez' Berry could have been in a band, Happy Mondays, for almost a decade despite the fact that his abilities extended to dancing badly and shaking the occasional maraca said a lot about the movement's attitude towards musicianship. It's not even as if anyone tried to disguise Bez's ineptitude. Originally listed as the group's percussionist, when the Mondays' second album was released the contributors' list began with 'Shaun Ryder - vocals' and ended with 'Bez - Bez.' That was his job; being himself. But then that was what Madchester was really all about.

However, there was a lot more to the Madchester scene than just music. The movement was a genuine cultural phenomenon that affected all media and even coloured the country's social history. And so here for your nostalgic enjoyment are just some of the things that Manchester had to answer for: cultural phenomena and fashions, people and places that illustrate the time and the place and without which the baggy boom might have been a mere whimper.

Tony Wilson

Variously recognised as a Cambridge graduate, TV presenter, documentary film-maker, game show host, nightclub owner and "twat" (according to Peter Hook), Anthony H Wilson is perhaps best known as the co-founder of Factory Records.

Setting the label up with band manager Alan Erasmus and designer Peter Saville, Wilson funded Factory's first release with £3,000 he'd been left by his mother. When he saw a return on that money, he knew he had enough to invest in a band he'd taken a liking to called Joy Division. Arranging a lunchtime meeting with the group's manager Rob Gretton, Wilson penned a contract on a napkin that was so generous towards Joy Division as to be almost ludicrous. So began Factory's policy of blending extreme generosity (the label's 18% royalty policy compared favourably with the industry standard of 12-15%) with naïveté that was as charming as it could be crippling.

Indeed, even when Factory was doing very good business during the early 1990s, the label's haphazard attitude towards cash meant that the local brewery was refusing to release beer to Wilson's Hacienda nightclub and the label's pressing plant didn't have enough money to buy vinyl. Of course, these problems were resolved. Indeed, it didn't seem to matter what trouble the label got into, it always managed to extricate itself. Somehow.

A lot of the time, it was the copious amounts of cash New Order earned for Factory that provided its means of escape. It would be wrong to get the idea that the label were a one-band outfit, however. Besides the hugely successful Happy Mondays, Factory's roster also featured austere funk masters A Certain Ratio, an early incarnation of Orchestral Manoeuvres In The Dark, Cabaret Voltaire and the Alan Erasmus-managed Durutti Column. Yes, they let bands slip though their fingers - James recorded two EPs for the label and then signed to Sire - but it's hard not to be impressed by Wilson's personal philosophy as summed up in an interview with *Vox* magazine in January 1992: "Shaun Ryder said to me a couple of years ago: 'Bet you wish you had The Stone Roses and not us, don't you? You'd make more money.' I said: 'Shaun, my own ego is: I want the most important group, not the most successful. If I had The Roses and not you, I'd be profoundly upset.'"

It's hard not to be impressed with Wilson's accomplishments away from Factory either. A contributor to ace current affairs programme *World*

In Action at an age when he ought probably to have been working as a runner, Wilson also ran the Russel Club and masterminded a music magazine programme for Granada TV called *So It Goes*. Reviews of the show tended to be unkind, particularly towards Wilson: it wasn't uncommon to see him referred to as a cunt in the music press. However, without the programme, it's doubtful whether local bands like Joy Division and the Buzzcocks would have got any exposure at all or that The Pistols and The Clash would ever have got on air north of Watford.

Even when Factory was fully up and running, Wilson continued to keep busy: an ITV business advice series, a gig hosting the Channel 4 spin-off of MTV game show *Remote Control*. If only he could have found a bit more time to look after the business side of running a record label. Factory's financial headaches posed particularly severe problems for New Order. In interviews, the band members claimed that whenever they were faced with a large tax demand, Wilson's response was to suggest that they go on a world tour. Responding to this claim on a recent Channel 4 *Top Ten* show about electronic music, the Factory boss said that the band got their own back on him by saying that they would only play five dates and one of those would have to be in Macclesfield. Whether or not any of this is true, Factory co-founder Peter Saville was under no illusions at all as to what was wrong with the company: "It was all down to a few basic points of business. Nobody wanted to play the businessman."

And in the end, for all the great music it produced, for its magnificent contribution to Manchester's nightlife and its many loveable idiosyncrasies (everything, from the records they released to the cat, had a catalogue number), an unwillingness to behave like grown-ups meant that on 23 November 1992, Britain's greatest ever independent record company filed for bankruptcy. However, only a fool or a communist would suggest that the final chapter of Factory Records has been written. Tony Wilson has already reactivated the label to promote his protégés The Space Monkeys and he has talked about fully resurrecting it. Even if it has shut down for good, we certainly haven't seen the last of Tony Wilson. He is after all, a person who, as recently as the year 2000, was still hosting an arts programme on the cultural cul-de-sac that is Carlton Television. If he could achieve that, who is to say a fully functioning Factory isn't a possibility?

Yes, it's hard to like him and almost impossible to love him, but life would not be as much fun if Anthony H Wilson was not around.

Paul Morley

If there's ever to be a poet laureate of music writing, it really ought to be Paul Morley. Although he could be as irritating as Tony Parsons and as controversial as Julie Burchill, Morley never gave the impression that he set out to be either on purpose. What's more, while the aforementioned pair proved that there was more to record reviewing than guff like 'Side two begins with a really punchy number,' Morley, by writing so passionately about the North-West, showed that a hack could actually be responsible for introducing a nation to its greatest gifts.

Paul Morley first attracted attention in the 1970s when he established himself as one of the few journos who could have a civilised conversation with Joy Division. After nearly getting into a fight with one of the correspondents from *Sounds*, the band had become rather edgy about talking to the press (to this day, New Order have a reputation, completely unfounded, for not giving interviews). Morley, however, not only got on with the group, he got beneath their dark exterior. As he recalled in the wonderful Radio One documentary (or, if you will, rockumentary) *Joy Division - I Remember When We Were Young*: "My favourite memory of Bernard was when I asked what he wanted to drink and he said a quadruple Pernod & Black. Now, that really did pierce the myth."

In the years that followed, Morley documented the emergence of Joy Division, the tragic demise of Ian Curtis and the formation and rise to high estate of New Order. He also wrote about other Manchester phenomena like the collapse of the Buzzcocks, the turmoil that was The Fall and the short, sweet career of The Smiths. He even dabbled with the idea of becoming a pop star himself, contributing weird lyrics and even weirder sleeve notes to JJ Jeckzalik's experimental outfit The Art Of Noise. All this and a gig editing the *NME*, where he caused quite a stir when he stuck Welwyn Garden City's finest Kim Wilde on the front cover.

Whether he wrote any more than other writers about the Madchester scene is a moot point since he certainly contributed to the grand, pretentious style in which hacks appraised the movement and its music. Morley was in particularly fine form when he came to write the sleeve notes for the *neworderstory* video: 'Where are New Order? They are at home, I presume. Or they are flying across the ocean. And they're right in the middle of this collection, their home from home, their flight from flight. But wherever they are, right now, they are, in their own special way, telling right from wrong, and indulging in slight extravaganzas.' Morley wasn't the worst culprit, however. When Happy Mondays released *Pills 'N' Thrills...*, the *NME* published a review that you needed a degree to understand. This wasn't an isolated incident by any means. Indeed, pretentious rock journalism was so common at the height of baggy that Radio One DJ Steve Wright featured a journo with delusions of grandeur amongst his cast of afternoon show comedy characters. And people still have a habit of talking bollocks when they recall the era today. Just check out what Tony Wilson said when asked to talk about his favourite Madchester track, Happy Mondays' 'Lazyitis' - "How do you explain to people that Sean Ryder is almost TS Eliot? *The Wasteland* is bits of other pies and 'Lazyitis' is a song which takes his mother saying to him as a child 'you've got lazyitis you have,' it takes one of the greatest songs of all time, 'Family Affair' by Sly & The Family Stone, and it also feeds in 'Ticket To Ride' by The Beatles. You've got these three songs extra, the song itself, and they twirl around each other, and at the end it becomes a 'round,' an English folk tradition." Folk music, Lennon, McCartney, Sly Stone, TS Eliot… and all this in a review of a song that's good but not *that* good.

Admittedly, Morley was better at the pretentious stuff than most of his rivals. While others used it to show off their education he used it to convey a sense that something epic and important was afoot in the North-West. The writer was also popularly perceived as an expert on what was going down. He was approached by Jonathan Ross to appear in a discussion on contemporary dance culture and ended up having a glass of water thrown in his face by a disgruntled club owner for his trouble. He was also hired to write and direct the awesome *neworderstory* and contributed memorably to a tribute to Morrissey during which he said that the former Smiths frontman should be awarded a Knighthood for writing 'We Hate It When Our Friends Become Successful.'

And he's still at it today. A writer for all manner of magazines, Morley occasionally pops up on *Late Review* and is a regular contributor to list programmes like the Channel 4 *Top Ten* series and the BBC's *I Love The '70s/The '80s/The Weekend Before Last* even though they are clearly beneath him. A little older now (his chins are beginning to multiply), he still sometimes veers into the pretentious (his first novel was called *Masturbation*) but his reputation as an incisive writer who shocks in spite of himself remains intact. Just check out his comments about Live Aid on Channel 4's *TV To Die For*. Attacking Bob Geldof's worthy endeavour has long been an easy way for a commentator to seem controversial. Morley, however, just said in a very matter-of-fact manner that the sad thing about the whole day was that it proved that music was no longer just about music - it was now about having a career.

Paul Morley. Journalist. Film-maker. Good friend to Joy Division. Chronicler of New Order and all that was Madchester. Occasional toss pot. Always good television. So when does he get his Knighthood?

Joe Bloggs

The strange thing about movements is the effect they have on the concept of individuality. When punk came along, people who felt they were outsiders were given a fantastic opportunity to hang out with lots of other people who were convinced they were outsiders. These kids who felt they didn't fit in perversely found themselves wearing a uniform of sorts: ripped jeans, stained slogan T-shirts and severe crew cuts. They would have liked to have thought they were being edgy, but they were sheep like everyone else. They just happened to be part of a different flock.

A similar thing happened with Madchester where teens said bollocks to the mundane, civilised world of their parents and immediately became arch-consumers. And as Malcolm McLaren and Vivian Westwood provided the punk world with its day-wear, so it was left to Shami Ahmed to provide Madchester's sartorial swagger. As the founder of Joe Bloggs, Ahmed helped create a range of clothes that were slobbish, smart and reassuringly expensive. Besides T-shirts bearing the company's label or a corruption of it, Joe Bloggs was particularly well known for its loose fit jeans. Yep, if you wanted a pair of denims that hung off your arse and had a bottom wide enough to hide a small dog under, Shami Ahmed was the man to see. "The jeans started with a 17-inch bottom," the entrepreneur remembers. "And the 17 inch went to 18 inch. And the 18 inch went to 19 inch." Ahmed's happy to point out that there were limits to these style excesses, though: "One time we made a pair of jeans with a 30 inch bottom but they were not that commercial."

Almost as shrewd as Ahmed having seen that there was money to be made out of smartening up scruffy Northern monkeys was the way in which he promoted his wears. Reluctant to pay people to endorse Joe Bloggs, Ahmed simply gave goods away to acts like Inspiral Carpets and Happy Mondays. When the bands appeared in magazine photo shoots wearing his clothes, Ahmed garnered publicity of a sort he couldn't have afforded. As good as the gear looked on the likes of Bez, it had to be said the Joe Bloggs wear in general looked considerably better in Hulme than it did in the Home Counties. As comedian Iain Lee recalled on the BBC's *I Love 1989*: "If you dressed in the baggy stuff in Slough you were a bit of a gyppo - a bit of a piker." On the same show, journalist John Robb observed that: "A year after Madchester was massive, Joe Bloggs seemed to be a millionaire, all power to him." A decade on, Shami Ahmed is now a Labour peer.

James Anderton

Now there's a name you probably haven't conjured with for a while. It's even possible that you'd completely wiped any memory of the former Chief of the Greater Manchester Police and his curmudgeonly, bearded face from your memory banks.

If you do remember him for anything it'll probably be the time that he went on Radio 4 and claimed that he was a prophet of God who conversed with the Lord on a daily basis. It was an amazing statement for a man in such a responsible position to make. It was even more remarkable that absolutely no action was taken against Anderton. When David Icke, a mere sports presenter, went on *Wogan* and made similar claims, he was vilified by all. But the only comment on Anderton came from *Spitting Image* who paired the clearly barking PC in a crime-fighting duo with the Almighty (Anderton: "All right, God, you guard the front windows, the back windows, the stairs and the fire escape. I'll just stand here and rant!")

There's more to James Anderton than this one outburst of idiocy. An investigating officer at the time of the Yorkshire Ripper murders, Anderton was in the unusual position of also being a suspect because he had an uncompromising attitude towards prostitutes (a lay preacher, he seemed to interpret *The Bible* in a distinctly Old Testament fashion) and bore a close resemblance to the man cited in witness reports (squint at a picture of Peter Sutcliffe and you'll see what people were getting at). As for his popularity in Manchester, that seemed to evaporate when, with the town's reputation as a party city increasing, the Greater Manchester Police launched a crackdown on anyone dealing in or using drugs. His reputation was further tarnished by the police's handling of the Strangeways Prison riots. (Anderton was in charge of the investigation into the upheaval, Operation Bastille.)

Knighted in 1990, Anderton retired from service one year later. His arrogance and smug manner went some way to ensuring that his name wouldn't be forgotten. However, Anderton had been such a dark spot on the face of Manchester, that he was also awarded a place in music history. In *neworderstory*, Bernard Sumner talks about how he'd tried to write a song about the Police Chief: "but it sounded corny." Nevertheless, you don't have to read between the lines of Electronic's album track 'Idiot Country' too far to see that Sumner did have it in him to attack the GMP's regime ('It's an open act of defiance/and it's aimed directly at you'). Anderton also came in for another, rather more obvious, kicking on 'God's Cop,' a track performed by Happy Mondays and written by Shaun Ryder, whose scruffy gear and messed-up mind disguised a social commentator so keen years later he achieved the rare feat for a pop star off royally pissing off the Pope.

Ecstasy

Ecstasy, or as it's more properly known MDMA, was produced first by German pharmaceutical giant Merck just prior to the First World War. Examined originally, believe it or not, for possible use in combat situations ("There's the enemy, lads. Let's go over and dance with them"), it was experimented with in the US in the 1940s, again with an eye to aiding the military effort. It wasn't until the 1970s that it surfaced in civilian America where psychiatrist Leo Zoff began to use E, or Adam as it was then known, to treat mental illness. The drug then found its way into New York's gay club scene. It had a particular influence on one Marc Almond who was in the city to record his first album with Soft Cell and would cryptically acknowledge the influence it had on the LP's sound in its title: *Non-Stop Erotic Cabaret* (he did the same thing with the follow-up, *Non-Stop Ecstatic Dancing*). From here the drug migrated to the Balearic Islands where it was discovered by blissed-out holidaying Brits.

Ecstasy's association with Madchester stems largely from the fact that it is a club drug and Manchester was the clubbing capital of the UK at the time. There were venues in London like Kinky Disco and Flying whose association with the Ibiza sound meant that the drug was recognised, but before the all-out blizzard of E hit Britain (it's now estimated that a million pills are consumed every weekend), Manchester was the place to get well and truly monkeyed.

Ecstasy also found its way into the music that was coming out of the city. There are, in fact, pretty 'out there' lyrics to be found on many of the records made at the time. The Mondays, though, not only used to sell E at

The Hacienda but they regularly took the drug while working on their second LP *Bummed*. Paul Ryder: "The songs weren't written on E but that swirling production, that was definitely E inspired. The newest songs of that album were 'Wrote For Luck' and 'Do It Better' with all the 'On one, have one' lyrics. No one outside of Manchester knew what it meant. We were going off in a new direction." E's greatest influence on the Madchester sound, however, is to be found on Primal Scream's 1991 LP *Screamadelica*. A record made largely on E (*Q*'s John Tobe comments that Bobby Gillespie's band were regulars at Flying throughout the recording of the album), it comes on like an album designed to be listened to by people taking the substance in question. Just look at the track listing: 'Movin' On Up,' 'Slip Inside This House,' 'Don't Fight It, Feel It,' 'Inner Flight,' 'Come Together,' 'Loaded,' 'Damaged,' 'I'm Comin' Down,' 'Higher Than The Sun,' 'Shine Like Stars.' Little wonder that Tobe describes it as 'a true clubbing concept album.'

The Strangeways Riots

Manchester's Strangeways Prison was guaranteed a place in the history of rock 'n' roll long before Ian Brown was sent there for threatening a flight attendant. Lending its name to The Smiths' final long-player, the prison, or more precisely its car park, is the place where drummer Steven Morris first met the other members of Joy Division. Morris: "I remembered thinking to myself, have they really just got back from holiday or have they been inside?"

In the spring of 1990, a fracas at the prison escalated into a riot which in turn led to a 23-day occupation of the facility by the prisoners. Quite what this had to do with the Madchester scene is simple - it was the closest thing baggy had to the Vietnam War. The Strangeways riots reflected the outside world, exposed the full extent of the baggy boom and influenced cultural affairs, accentuating the aforementioned antipathy towards James Anderton and his police force, and leading people like Shaun Ryder to acknowledge their disgust in song.

If there is one image of the Strangeways riots that's burnt into the nation's collective memory, it is of convicts performing the monkey dance made famous by the Mondays' Bez on the prison rooftops. In that moment, it became apparent that Madchester had managed to reach everybody. You could be a lifer, sent down in the days when Gilbert O'Sullivan was riding high but the chances were you still knew who Ian Brown was.

It was also true to say that a lot of people on the outside could sympathise with the behaviour of those inside. Indeed, with the Greater Manchester Police making it harder and harder for people to have a good time in Manchester, some disgruntled clubbers would have loved to have indulged in the same police-baiting activities as the rioters.

However, by far the most revealing thing about the riots was that they showed how closely the lines were drawn. Look at the men who occupied the prison rooftops and then study a picture of the Mondays and you'll see little difference. Indeed, when the last four prisoners were brought down in a cherry picker, an event that was shown live in the closing minutes of the BBC news, it could just as easily have been Shaun Ryder smiling defiantly. In fact, if you look at the similar backgrounds the band mates and the cons shared, they could very easily have been one another. Cut from the same cloth, the fact that one bunch had been handed a magic ticket while the others had been handed down heavy sentences was as tragic as the message was clear - in Madchester, the lunatics really had taken over the asylum.

The Word

'In the beginning, there was *The Word*,' but there was nothing holy about Channel 4's early 1990s entertainment extravaganza, aside from the fact that it was hosted by one Terry Christian. Originally airing at 6 p.m. on Friday evenings, the show promised the best bands, top celebrity interviews and eye-opening features. What it delivered were largely sub-standard live performances shot in a nauseating, swirling camera style, star chat spots that were completely undone by Christian's mannered style and the chance to see everything from a man having his penis surgically enlarged to a dog being castrated.

It was risqués items like this that led to the show being moved to 11 p.m., after which we were able to enjoy such sights as hostess Amanda De Cadenet measuring 'Marky' Mark Whalberg's chest, Jim Rose's circus freaks sticking nails through their faces and Oliver Reed getting pissed up in his dressing room before performing 'Wild Thing' with Ned's Atomic Dustbin. The shift to late night also meant we had to endure the Hopeless Hopefuls - a bunch of credulous teens who were so desperate for TV exposure they'd do anything from snogging OAPs to drinking their own sick.

The Word nailed its Madchester credentials to the mast in the first show which kicked off with the Mondays performing 'Judge Fudge' and was then dominated by Christian's terse delivery and impossible-to-impress manner. The connection grew stronger with the booking of more and more baggy bands and the eminently wise decision to replace the original theme music with a remix of 808 State's 'In Yer Face.'

Yes, there was some talent involved: Jonathan Ross' brother Paul produced; future Radio One DJ Jo Whiley was the booker; and later series were co-presented by sharp Swindon comedian Mark Lamarr. And there were highlights: like the live British TV debuts of Nirvana and Oasis (the former were booked at Jo Whiley's behest, the latter at Terry Christian's), The La's blazing through 'There She Goes,' a performance from Rage Against The Machine that ended in a near riot, Rod Hull and Emu wrestling with Snoop Doogy Dogg. Best of all, however, was the moment when Lamarr took Shabba Ranks to task over his homophobic posturing and so became the first person in the history of the world to talk back to the ragga star. After it was dragged off air, nobody missed *The Word* but everyone remembered it. And compared to some of the dross that followed it, like the ghastly *Girlie Show*, *The Word* resembled *The Ascent Of Man*.

The Hacienda

Ask people to name the world's most famous nightclub and it's a pretty good bet that they'll say The Hacienda. Sure, you might get the odd smart sod who'll say Ministry Of Sound or 1990s acid venues like The Futurama and Spectrum, but you'll be amazed how many will quote the name of a venue that has long since ceased to exist.

Formerly a yacht showroom, The Hacienda was purchased by Tony Wilson with money raised from New Order's record sales. Recalls Wilson: "The idea was we'd pay royalties to Manchester. Because without the live culture of this town, Joy Division would never have been what they were and New Order would never have been what they are." It was a noble, romantic gesture but one that did not sit too well with Factory's top act. "I was living in a fucking council house," Bernard Sumner recalls in the *neworderstory* documentary, "and we were pouring ten grand a month into The Hacienda. That is ridiculous and wrong." Peter Hook was also pretty nonplussed as he'd just bought a Jaguar but, because of the nightclub subsidies, he couldn't afford to put petrol in it. And as for Steven

Morris: "On the opening night of the Hacienda, I had to pay to get in. Gillian's sister used to get in free on the guest list by impersonating Gillian. And it took me nine years to get one free drink. I'm not a bitter man, I'm not a bitter man."

The Hacienda certainly caused New Order its fair share of hassle (the band's problems multiplied when they pumped money into a bar, Dry, and then helped purchase and refurbish the Factory office), but it was hard to argue that their endeavours weren't worth it. Even Peter Hook sees that the venue has done good things for the city: "I think it's important to show that you're willing to put something back in." And as for the regulars, well they certainly weren't complaining. "There was no club anywhere else in the world like The Hacienda, where you were going to get in for £3.50," claims Terry Christian. The venue where Madonna made her live TV debut (she guested on a special edition of *The Tube* and so impressed Peter Hook that he offered her £50 to perform again later the same evening; Ms Ciccone impolitely declined), the club and its many events (Nude Night where couples would strip one another on the dance floor, the self-explanatory Gay Night) became institutions. And as going to The Hacienda became a rite of passage, so the club became so big that, when the time came to celebrate its tenth anniversary, the festivities took place not in the club itself but in Amsterdam where a rare live performance from New Order was followed by the sight of a stripper shoving a Swiss Roll where the sun doesn't shine. The message was clear: the Hacienda was less an actual place than a state of mind. And between 1988 and 1992, it was a mindset that an enormous number of people shared.

Infamous for having the bass turned up so high you could hear it three miles away, the club's dedication to hedonism didn't sit well with everyone. If you weren't part of the scene a lot of what took place at The Hacienda sounded just plain daft. As comedian Johnny Vegas recalled on *I Love 1989*: "Certain cooler people went over to Manchester and came back with tales of clubs full of happy people drinking water. And we'd be all like: 'Ah, you're having a laugh! Get away! What, is it like that episode of *Battlestar Galactica* where they lure them down to that planet and then eat them? It can't be that good?'"

For true Madchester devotees, however, The Hacienda was the only place to be seen. Sadly, the scallys' fun was soured as the venue developed a reputation for guns and drugs and Wilson was forced to suspend trading on many occasions. And then, as the baggy boom burst and the

Factory ship finally sank, the venue was sold off and demolished. Nothing, however, could wipe out people's memories of The Hacienda and if you look around closely enough, you can still find evidence of its nation-spanning reputation. To this end, walk down Bridge Road in Welwyn Garden City until you reach a road sign situated opposite the Nabisco factory. There you will find a dark oblong streak, the remnants of a sticker that has faded from pristine white to charcoal grey. Peer at it closely, though, and you will read the following slogan: The Hacienda Must Be Built. In case you're wondering, I didn't stick it there, but the fact that, in a safe, comfortable commuter suburb like leafy Welwyn Garden City, somebody else did still brings a smile to my face.

Morley, Wilson, Joe Bloggs, The Hacienda... Madchester wouldn't have been Madchester without them. The party proper's over now, of course. When did it end? No one's sure. As we'll see, you can persuasively argue that it really didn't finish at all. But whether or not you see Brit Pop as the bastard son of baggy, there's no denying that some of the institutions that made it have changed utterly. The Hacienda has been bulldozed. Factory Records has reached the end of the line. And Manchester United, whose players couldn't hit a cow's arse with a banjo back in 1988, have scooped the Champions League, a clutch of Premierships and any number of FA Cups.

It's a shame, isn't it?

3. Forefathers

There was a Manchester scene prior to 1988. As long ago as the 1960s, Herman's Hermits, Freddie & The Dreamers and The Hollies were racking up impressive singles sales on both sides of the Atlantic. By the time baggy had swung by, there weren't too many teens taking their lead from Peter Noone, Freddie Garity or Graham Nash.

Any number of local 1970s acts contributed to the sound and excitement of the late 1980s. Magazine, Joy Division, Eater, A Certain Ratio, Slaughter & The Dogs, Vini Reilly… you'll hear echoes of all of them in the music of Madchester. What follows are profiles of five key acts. Some contributed greatly to the noise that would later emerge from the North-West. Others not only laid down blueprints but also sculpted the scene by actively participating in it. Put simply, these are bands without whom there wouldn't have been either a Madchester scene or this book. So blame them.

Buzzcocks

Formed 1976. Split up 1987. Reformed 1993.

Key Personnel: Howard Devoto (guitar/vocals), Pete Shelley (guitar/vocals), Steve Diggle (bass/guitar/vocals), John Maher (drums), Steve Garvey (guitar).

As Charterhouse produced Genesis so Bolton Institute Of Higher Learning gave the world the Buzzcocks. Taking their name from one of the bands in ITV drama series *Rock Follies*, the group was brought together by a 'musicians wanted' flyer stapled to the college notice board by Pete Shelley. Convinced the poster had something to do with the Institute's Sexual Deviant Society, aspiring singer Howard Devoto immediately contacted the guitarist.

With Diggle and Maher also on board, the group began to make music. In the months that followed the Buzzcocks ensured themselves a place in pop history by i) securing The Sex Pistols their first concert outside of London and ii) helping local act Joy Division find a name (Shelley's suggestion, The Stiff Kittens, was adopted, then swiftly ditched), a sound and a debut gig. Pete Shelley: "There was this great mystique about forming a band. We were just making it up as we went along but Ian Curtis asked for advice and we were only too happy to help."

In between making rock 'n' roll history, the group found time to cut their first record, the independently-released 'Spiral Scratch' EP. Fabulously influential, it featured both the brilliant 'Boredom' (a song Sooty and Sweep surreally performed on Tony Wilson's *So It Goes*) and Devoto's first and last vocal performance with the band. In an interview with Channel 4, the singer explained that he quit because: "We'd done what we'd set out to do. We'd made a record. That was a landmark. Now it was time to move on." Moving on meant forming the marvellous Magazine. A mere four years later, however, Howard Devoto would leave the music industry forever.

Devoto's departure left Pete Shelley to handle the singing and songwriting duties. Since the guitarist had a slightly effeminate voice, he didn't seem best suited to the job of fronting what was ostensibly a punk outfit. But by marrying his distinctive vocals with songs that were more concerned with splitting up than spitting, heartaches than head butts, Shelley ensured that both he and his band stood out.

It wasn't just their combination of harsh guitar and sincere sensitivity that made the Buzzcocks hard to ignore. While most of their contemporaries struggled to survive beyond their first gig, the band enjoyed bona fide success. A critically-acclaimed album *Another Music In A Different Kitchen* (a play on a track from *Evita* which, coincidentally, starred Rock Folly Julie Covington) was followed by a string of hit singles such as 'What Do I Get,' 'Promises' and the number 12 smash 'Ever Fallen In Love (With Someone You Shouldn't Have).' Then, just as it looked like the outfit might be about to set off on a sensational pop adventure, Shelley started experimenting with LSD, the other band members wanted in on the writing front and the chart excursions began to get shorter. Come 1978, Pete Shelley was working as a solo artist.

Fifteen years passed before the group drifted back together to capitalise on the punk nostalgia boom. The subsequent tour went so swimmingly that they're still on the road today - portly, grey and in their forties, sure, but with a CV of songs that kick the ass of most modern efforts. But while the group's advancing years have lent fresh poignancy to 'Ever Fallen In Love...,' the teen angst having now given way to mid-life crisis, the sight of fat, sweaty, middle-aged men belting out 'Orgasm Addict' is just plain wrong.

The Buzzcocks' influence was as profound as their time together was relatively brief. If you can't imagine their sound, think of what Sham 69 might have been like had they been led not by Jimmy Pursey but by Radiohead's Thom Yorke. And for examples of the impact they made on Madchester, don't look to Happy Mondays. Instead, fish out The Stone Roses' 'Sally Cinnamon' or 'I Wanna Be Adored,' or The Inspiral Carpets' 'This Is How It Feels.' Shaun Ryder has said his hero is Johnny Rotten and his music is clearly informed by the same obsessions with hedonism, hate and having a laugh. It was Pete Shelley, though, who made it cool for good-time boys like Ian Brown to also sing about the bad times. And if there hadn't been introspection to go with the high times, Madchester might have been over as quickly as the blink-and-you-missed-it Stourbridge boom.

Essential Song: 'Ever Fallen In Love (With Someone You Shouldn't Have)' Forget the Fine Young Cannibals' lukewarm cover version; this is how bitterness and frustration is meant to sound. As for the magnificent title, it was taken from a line from the Brando/Sinatra musical *Guys & Dolls*.

Essential Album: *Singles Going Steady - Another Music In A Different Kitchen* is a great record and *Love Bites* has things to recommend it. However, it was as a singles band that the Buzzcocks really shone and, as such, this is the only compilation worth owning.

Joy Division

Formed 1977. Reformed as New Order 1980.

Key Personnel: Ian Curtis (vocals/guitar), Bernard Albrecht (guitar/keyboards), Peter Hook (bass), Steven Morris (drums).

Fifteen-year-old Peter Hook had just arrived home from a week's holiday in Torquay when he heard that The Sex Pistols and The Clash were to play Manchester Free Trade Hall. Borrowing the 50p entrance fee from his mum, Hook and schoolmate Bernard Albrecht soon found themselves with tickets for a gig whose status would become so legendary that if all the people who claimed to have been there had actually attended, they'd have had to have held the concert at the Maracana. With their eyes opened and their minds blown, the two friends resolved to form their own band as quickly as possible.

"Curiously," Hook told the BBC, "it wasn't a musical impulse that got us started. We just wanted to have a good time." It was because of this ethos that the budding musicians recruited not the best singer they could find but one of the blokes they used to go to concerts with. It was pure luck that the man they chose, Ian Curtis, was a visionary genius.

Curtis' first contribution to the band was to recruit a drummer, oft-expelled schoolboy Steven Morris. Morris: "They seemed to like my ability to go boom-bang at fairly regular intervals." It was also the singer who insisted on a six-month period of rehearsal, who cribbed ideas from Buzzcock Pete Shelley and who abused his office privileges to find the group gigs - all this while trying to cope with the pressures of epilepsy, married life and imminent fatherhood. This isn't to say that Curtis did all the hard work. Hooky: "I used to have to drive the bleedin' van." However, it was the lead singer who accosted local media personality and aspiring record company boss Tony Wilson at a 'battle of the bands' contest hosted by the labels Stiff and Chiswick and berated him about not doing anything for bands like Warsaw, as the act was then known. The torrent of abuse Wilson copped was quite incredible. Wilson: "He walked over to me and said: 'you're a fuckin' cunt!'" But it, together with Warsaw's breathtaking performance that night, secured the group a record contract with Wilson's Factory label. Warsaw also discovered their first diehard fan, Rob Gretton, the DJ at the venue and the man who would soon become the band's manager.

Now that they had a record deal, a loyal following and an adoring manager, Joy Division, as they had rebranded themselves, could set about making serious music. For a generation raised on the likes of Radiohead and Nirvana, it's hard to understand just how bleak the noise Joy Division made was. There was no fashionable pessimism where Ian Curtis was concerned. His were songs about epic loss, grotesque betrayal, crippling unworthiness. This didn't stem from an unappealing, 'why does it always rain on me' strain of self-pity, though. Curtis had real things to be upset about, namely a marriage that wasn't working and an illness that complicated even the very easy things in life.

Although Curtis' dark visions were far from inauthentic, Joy Division could still have slipped into self-indulgent misanthropy had they not had such a talented team around them. Besides Wilson and Gretton, there was Factory co-founder Peter Saville to cloak the group's single and album sleeves in serene, utterly cool coldness. A local artist, Saville had bumped into Tony Wilson at a Patti Smith concert and asked him if he had any work going. Asked to design a poster for Wilson's Factory club (the forerunner to The Hacienda), Saville spent so long at his desk that the work wasn't completed until after the club had closed. Nevertheless, Wilson was won over and hired Saville to work on Joy Division's cover work; an inspired decision since the young graduate's ideas were in synch with those of the band who had no great desire to appear on their album covers and who felt the sleeves should give as little away about Joy Division as possible.

Besides Saville, there was also music journalist Paul Morley, who freely admits that he subconsciously contributed to the act's association with misanthropy because he wrote most of his gig reviews: "at 4am, when your mother was shouting at you to keep the noise down and you'd just found out your girlfriend didn't want to speak to you anymore." The crew was further rounded out by Factory's in-house producer Martin Hannett and photographer Kevin Cummins, a man whose knack for capturing the sadness that surrounded the band included not only snapping them in the midst of the most ugly parts of Manchester's sprawling metropolis (principally Hulme and Stockport) but also choosing mildly melancholic dates on which to shoot them (the group's most celebrated set of photos was taken on January 6, the last day of Christmas). While Wilson, Saville, Cummins and Co. might have played a little too much on Joy Divison's miserablist tag, the end result wasn't a commercial curmudgeonliness but an inscrutable sheen that gave a truly epic feel to the band's angst. What's more, in their packaging of Joy Division, Factory never undercut the comforting decade-spanning central message that the band sent out, a reassurance to anyone outside of the party scene that if you weren't having as good a time as everyone else, that was okay. That was valid. You weren't an asshole. The problem was them, not you.

This acceptance of outsiders explains why Joy Division developed an incredibly large and loyal constituency. It wasn't a following of the same size and ferocity as The Pistols' - a fact that became quite apparent when debut album *Unknown Pleasures* stalled at number 71 - but you can guarantee that those that bought the LP listened to it a thousand times, dissecting Curtis' lyrics with a scalpel. The band themselves weren't too impressed with the piece (Sumner still complains that Joy Division went into the studio with a good album but it got lost because the production was, in his words, "a bit timid") but then artists never were the best judges of their work. Over twenty years on, *Unknown Pleasures* is still fraught, frightening and truly fantastic.

Although it garnered great reviews, *Unknown Pleasure*'s lowly chart position and the failure of the singles 'Transmission' and 'Atmosphere' did little to lighten Curtis' mood. Keen to push through the disappointment and keep expanding their fan base, the group embarked on an intense tour of the UK. The time also seemed right for them to chance their arm in America. But with his epilepsy now complicated by clinical depression and his marriage collapsing, Ian Curtis' time was up. On the morning of Sunday, 18 May 1980, Joy Divison's lead singer was discovered with a noose around his neck.

Tony Wilson was in a suite at Granada Television editing an edition of *World In Action* when he heard the news. "A phone call came and it was Rob. I said: 'Rob, I'm in the middle of editing a *World In Action* for tomorrow. Don't disturb me.' He said: 'I just thought you should know...' whatever. I told the editor I'd be back in thirty minutes. It's one of things where I can barely remember driving over to Rob's house but it was incredible, when I came out of Rob's house twenty minutes later, the way my car was parked - sideways in the middle of the road - the way you park a car when you're in a state of shock, is so different from the way you park a car normally. It's like: 'nothing now matters, so I'll park my car in the middle of the road because nothing is relevant.'" Bernard Albrecht also recalls receiving a call from the band's manager. "Rob rang and said: 'Ian's killed himself.' I said: 'You mean he's tried to kill himself.' And he said: 'No, he's done it. He's dead.' And the room just span round." Steven Morris, meanwhile, sums up his feelings up in a single sentence: "On Sunday night, I was turning up my trousers, on Monday morning, I woke up screaming." The tragedy was compacted when, a week after the suicide of the success-hungry Curtis, Joy Division's single 'Love Will Tear Us Apart' entered the UK top 20. Shortly afterwards, the band's second album, *Closer*, reached the top ten. A live album, *Still*, also performed impressively.

Whether it was due to this hard-earned success or a simple sense of solidarity, Hook, Morris and Bernard Sumner (as Albrecht had rechristened himself) decided that they would continue to make music. Out of Joy Division, another, some might say a better, band was born, New Order. Tasteless as it might sound, any discussion of Joy Division and their music is tainted by the fact that, were it not for the death of Ian Curtis, we might not have 'Blue Monday,' 'Elegia,' 'Regret,' 'Temptation,' 'True

Faith,' 'Thieves Like Us,' etc. Would Joy Division have gone on to become New Order without so spectacular and final an epiphany?

I'd like to think that the answer is 'yes.' After all, it was Ian Curtis who introduced the band to the electronic music of Can and Kraftwerk, who suggested Albrecht buy his first keyboard (costing £2,000, it came in kit form), who faded out The Pistols' thrash and faded in the synthesiser swash. What's more, New Order themselves have acknowledged Curtis' contribution to their musical progression, both consciously in interviews and subconsciously in the magnificent clip for their 1985 single 'The Perfect Kiss.' Directed by Jonathan Demme (*Something Wild*, *The Silence Of The Lambs*, *Philadelphia*), the promo shows the band cutting the track in a studio. It's a brilliantly straightforward performance video that achieves greatness in a fleeting moment when, as Hooky rides his bass, a thin pale figure appears reflected in the glass behind him. The man in question is probably just an engineer (you can see another one standing behind Bernard Sumner). However, there's no denying that he bares an uncanny resemblance to a certain Ian Curtis. Indeed, it's almost as if the band's former lead singer has come back to check on how his boys are doing. And judging from the way he groves along to the track, he's really liking what he hears. Of course, you could claim that there's something a little tasteless, even tacky about this - at least you could if the band in question wasn't New Order. As it is, since the moment occurs in a video made by a group that are as hard to convince as they are impossible to fool, it feels exactly the way it should do - truly heartfelt, understatedly epic, completely sincere, utterly embraceable.

Essential Song: 'Love Will Tear Us Apart.' "The most beautiful song ever written," Kurt Cobain.

Essential Album: *Closer*. Edges out the also excellent *Unknown Pleasures* on account of its ennobling bleakness and magnificent array of tracks. "Beautiful desolation" was how astronaut Buzz Aldrin described the Moon after landing on it. He could just as well have been talking about this album.

New Order

Formed 1980.

Key Personnel: Bernard Sumner (guitar/keyboards/vocals), Peter Hook (bass/vocals/keyboards), Steven Morris (drums/keyboards/sequencers), Gillian Gilbert (guitar/keyboards/sequencers).

It's traditional when talking about the birth of New Order to use the words 'Joy,' 'Division,' 'phoenix' and 'ashes.' So strong is this tradition, in fact, that I will make absolutely no effort to break from it. And lo! It came to pass that New Order sprung like a phoenix from the ashes of its former incarnation, Joy Division. And in that brief instant, the most important pioneers of the post-punk era became leading exponents of electronic dance music. Or so the legend would have us believe. In truth, the rise and rise of New Order is a story every bit as bizarre as the myths that have come to enshroud this truly fantastic band.

When he was informed of the suicide of his friend and Joy Division lead singer Ian Curtis, bass player Peter Hook's immediate thought was: "The bastard. I'm not going to get to America!" In the years subsequent to Curtis' passing, the group's other members, together with manager Rob Gretton and Factory Records owner Tony Wilson, developed a feeling of 'friendly annoyance' towards their colleague's passing. "Ian got out," remarks Wilson, "He left us with all the hard work to do. He should have gone through the shit with us." Hook is even more blunt. Asked in 1994 who the laziest member of New Order was, he commented: "Ian Curtis - he hasn't done anything for years." (Hook was also pretty up front when it came to the tricky subject of exploiting Curtis' death: "I'd have been happier if they had cashed in on it. I mean, why not? The basic plan with Ian was that he wanted the group to succeed, so if he's up there somewhere now, I don't think he'd give a monkey's about cashing in as long as Joy Division was heard by as many people as possible. But the thing is, Factory's too stupid to cash in on things like that. If Shaun Ryder had killed himself they couldn't bleedin' cash in on that. I know that, I take it for granted.")

To say the death of Curtis, arguably the most charismatic performer of his generation, left a void is sickening understatement. As for who would win the singer sweepstake, Hook, Sumner and Morris were so keen to avoid vocal duties, Tony Wilson toyed with recruiting A Certain Ratio's Simon Topping. In the end, however, it was Sumner who bit the bullet for the simple reason that, while none of the band found it easy to play and sing simultaneously, as the guitarist, he played less than the rhythm section.

Besides finding a new vocalist, the band thought it would be a good idea to give themselves a new name ("We were keen to avoid becoming Joy Division II," says Steven Morris). Black September, Barney & The JDs, The Sun Valley Dance Band and The Witch Doctors Of Zimbabwe all made the short lists, but in the end New Order won out (an unfortunate choice given that, like Joy Division, it had definite Nazi connotations). Alterations aside, a strong relationship continued to exist between New Order and their former self. The band's first single, 'Ceremony,' and its B-side, 'In A Lonely Place,' were both written by Ian Curtis (a fact that was lost on some music journalists who criticised Sumner for having only a fraction of his predecessor's songwriting talent). A further connection existed in the shape of Gillian Gilbert who was drafted into the group at Rob Gretton's insistence. "It was Rob's master stroke," reminisces Wilson, "not to bring anybody new into the group. And so he recruited Gillian who was Steven's girlfriend." More pertinently, Gilbert had played guitar with Joy Division at Liverpool Eric's one evening when Sumner hurt his hand. By bringing in Gillian, Gretton changed the band a lot while actually changing it very little.

With the line-up complete, New Order began to make serious music. Debut album *Movement* was greeted with stifled enthusiasm by the music press as was follow-up single 'Everything's Gone Green.' An ambitious experiment in electronic music, 'Everything's Gone Green' paved the way for the record which would break the band worldwide. In March 1983, Factory released a single in a peculiar, Peter Saville-designed, floppy disc-style packaging. 'Blue Monday' (which shares its name but absolutely nothing else with a song by Fats Domino) went on to become the biggest selling 12' of all time, a distinction it continues to hold even in these dance obsessed days. More impressive than its three million plus sales was the new sound the song brought to the fore. Only lazy journos dared describe 'Blue Monday' as 'boredom with a beat.' At a time when disco music meant The Bee Gees and KC & The Sunshine Band, New Order offered up something vivid and exciting, something Echo & The Bunnymen's Ian McCulloch would later describe as "intelligent dance music." The chart success of follow-up 'Confusion,' produced by New York legend Arthur Baker, proved 'Blue Monday' was anything but a fluke.

There was more to New Order than great dance music, however. Evidence of this was captured on the band's second album *Power, Corruption & Lies*. From jangly guitar pop ('Age Of Consent') to early dance trance ('Ecstasy), from incidental masterpieces ('Leave Me Alone') to bittersweet ballads ('Your Silent Face'), New Order did them all and they did them in a way that was all their own. Such was the group's agreement with Factory, they didn't need to release singles off albums or actively promote their records. New Order did what they liked, when they liked. The downside of this were irregular payments, whopping tax demands and an inspired but ill-advised commitment to Factory sponsored nightclub The Hacienda. The upside was singles like 'Thieves Like Us' and a fabulous third album, 1985's *Low Life*.

Low Life teed New Order up to fulfil Tony Wilson's prophecy that, within five years, New Order would be on a par with Pink Floyd and would be shifting millions of units in America. But with the dream within their grasp, New Order hit a dry spell. Singles like 'Shellshock' (recorded for the John Hughes film *Pretty In Pink*) and 'State Of The Nation' paled in comparison to earlier efforts. People were also pretty underwhelmed by album number four, *Brotherhood*. What can now be appreciated as a brave blend of acoustic, acid-house and Lou Reed rip-offs was simply too obscure for the audience of 1986. Entering the chart disappointingly at number 9, *Brotherhood* fell from sight two weeks later.

Then in 1987, New Order very quietly became a pop group.

The release of the retrospective *Substance* and the single 'True Faith' opened a new chapter in the life of New Order. This change was also marked by the band's air play shift from John Peel's mumblin' around midnight slot to daytime Radio One. No more would New Order be confined to the independent charts and the *NME*. Now they could be found miming on *Top Of The Pops* and answering tough questions about their favourite ice-cream in *Smash Hits*. The move to the mainstream was completed with 1989's dance-centric album *Technique* and 'World In Motion,' the 1990 England World Cup song and the band's first (and only) number one single.

No sooner had New Order scaled their Everest than the wheels began to come off. An epic promotional tour led to a rest & relaxation session so long, it looked as if *Technique* was going to be the last New Order album ever released. Although a split was never officially announced, the members spent more and more time on solo projects. Sumner started Electronic with Johnny Marr, Hook formed Revenge (and later Monaco) and Steven and Gillian became, appropriately enough, The Other Two. The band's future looked even more uncertain when, in 1991, Factory Records announced that it was to close. Ten years on, label owner Wilson still harbours dreams of relaunching Factory. If he does, however, it will be without New Order. For while the Factory ship was going down, New Order did what they'd said they'd never do - they moved to London!

Signing to London Records in 1992, the fruits of New Order's relationship with their new label have been disappointing to date. An inconsistent first album *Republic* was followed by an unnecessary second compilation *(The Best Of) New Order* and a horrific remix release, *(The Rest Of) New Order*. However, you only need to listen to the band's first London single, the truly majestic 'Regret' to realise why when it was announced at the 1999 *Q* Awards that the band were working on their seventh album proper, it was something to get genuinely excited about.

Two years later, and anticipation had turned to dread. With the record taking longer and longer to lick, New Order seemed to be preparing their fans for a major let-down. A first listen to *Get Ready*, however, proved that we had nothing to worry about. That it's immediately apparent that this is a New Order release was considered a sign of weakness by some critics but there's no lack of inventiveness here. All the band have done is to continue to progress musically while staying true to their unique epic, intimate sound. It should also be said that there's a wonderful feeling to the project as a whole. Whatever the relative merits of *Republic*, there was a certain sensation that the group were banging it out to demand rather than making music because they wanted to. *Get Ready*, though, comes on like a labour of love. There are even elements of rediscovery, of the band remembering why they got together in the first place, of Hooky remembering that he has a bass to ride and of Steven remembering that he has things to hit. Of course, all the great records that have gone before are bound to make any new New Order album feel like a bit of a disappointment. You wish more albums disappointed the way *Get Ready* does.

New Order aren't the most talented musicians in the world. They've never claimed to be. As Sumner once told the *NME*: "If you asked me to play an E minor, I wouldn't have a fucking clue." The band make their music in a peculiar fashion. Stephen Hague, John Robie and the other producers they've worked with freely admit that they aren't too sure how New Order make things happen. So haphazard a style tempts fate and when New Order get it wrong they sound ridiculous (to wit 'Shellshock': 'When we walk through open doorways/counting time in one or more ways'). But when they get it right (viz. the last line of the sublime 'Your Smiling Face': 'You caught me at a bad time/so why don't you piss off'), they are the most cherishable pop commodity we possess.

New Order are a band that exist on their own terms. As Tony Wilson has said: "In a world where nobody does what they want to do, New Order do just that." It's hard to know who's jammier - them or us?

Essential Song: 'Blue Monday.' It's not just hard to imagine where New Order might be without this glorious monument to electronic music (legend has it that the drum beat was born by accident during a programming session), you really don't know whether we'd have the throbbing dance scene we currently enjoy had Hook, Sumner and Co. not decided to rip off Kraftwerk and Sylvester simultaneously. Since few of the late 1980s bands could afford to use Fairlights, its contribution to the Manchester scene is tangential (the title inspired the Happy Mondays' choice of name), but its influence upon global music is beyond question.

Essential Album: *Technique*. Fans might argue that *Power, Corruption & Lies* is a better album, but it's *Technique* that marks New Order out from the other legendary Manchester acts because it proves that not only did they inspire the scene, they were actively involved with it. Indeed, while tracks like 'Loveless' rival the best of The Stone Roses' output, the dance-driven 'Vanishing Point' (which doubled as the theme tune to factory floor drama *Making Out*) shaped not only the styling of 808 State but went some way towards creating that which we now know as the Ibiza Sound. And what's more, like the movement's very best offerings, it still sounds light years ahead of the game. Not bad for a bunch of old Bezs.

The Fall

Formed 1977.

Key Personnel: Mark E Smith (vocals/guitar) and a cast of thousands.

It's hard to know what to make of Fall founder Mark E Smith. On the one hand, he is the man who celebrated winning an *NME* lifetime achievement award by telling that nice Jo Whiley to fuck off, who punched his girlfriend and keyboard player Julia Nagle in New York (a crime for which he nearly went to jail) and who described John Lennon as "the biggest spaz ever." On the other, the former office worker is a bit of a traditionalist (he still drinks in his local Catholic club and always stays in the

Columbia Hotel when he visits London), is somewhat old fashioned (he has a habit of asking journalists who interview him whether they are currently 'courting') and isn't scared of showing his sensitive side. During a recent 'Cash For Questions' session with *Q*, he was openly moved by an e-mail from reader Daniel Wilson. 'Smith,' wrote Wilson, 'your fans are concerned about you. Are you in a never-ending depression or should we mind our own business?' A genuinely choked Smith replied 'I appreciate your concern but don't worry about me, I'm fine. Thank you very much.'

It's also easy to look at The Fall's record sales (14 chart singles including a cover of The Kinks favourite 'Victoria' that made the top 40, a handful of top-20 albums) and leap to the wrong conclusions. For while they've never threatened the multi-Platinum status of Take That, the fact The Fall have shifted any units at all might have come as a great disappointment to Smith who seemed to have created the band as a sort of anti-pop group. And the fact that the self-confessed miserable bastard has grown more miserable with each passing year underpins another contradiction because, for all their misanthropy, it's hard not to have a place in your heart for The Fall.

If there's one thing everyone knows about Smith's band it is that they've had a million and one members. The more famous faces to have appeared in the line-up include the Hanley brothers, Steve and Paul, Gavin Friday who later scored motion pictures such as *In The Name Of The Father*, Smith's American wife Brix (who left him for classical violinist Nigel Kennedy) and Mark Radcliffe's wing-man Marc 'Lard' Riley. The group are also well known for having been signed to countless record labels, for releasing a new album every five minutes and for having a musical style that is notoriously difficult to pin down. You find the word Mancabilly being bandied about a lot in reviews but that doesn't cover the vast majority of their output. Miscellaneous might be a better term.

While his demeanour can sometimes suggest that he doesn't play well with others, it was only fitting that Smith should be given a ticket to his home town's greatest ever party. Actually, Madchester ushered in a period of unprecedented success for The Fall. 'Victoria,' 'White Lightning' and the 'Big New Prinz' double single all charted respectably, as did the 1991 LP *Shift Work*. What's more, Smith, a man who positively thrived on his image as an outsider, found himself in the unusual position of being asked to collaborate, first with dance kings Coldcut on the excellent 'Telephone

Thing' and then with fellow Mancunians Inspiral Carpets on their re-recording of 'I Want You.'

As important as Smith's musical contribution to Madchester was, the things he and The Fall represented had a far bigger impact on the baggy boom. A band that had refused to play the music industry game, that had made no attempt to push itself, that had seen music as an end in itself, The Fall were an object lesson to North-West musicians in how to put across a 'fuck you' attitude. Rather ironically, the pissed-off, politicised ranting that was the cornerstone of Smith's songwriting found no place in the world of The Roses and Mondays. However, it was The Fall frontman who subconsciously suggested that Shaun Ryder should always sport a sneer and that The Roses should enter contract disputes carrying pots of paints. And when disappointed parents started to pressure their sons into swapping their guitars for nice bank jobs, the kids only had to cite Mark E Smith (a man who'd be in a band forever and had got by, even without any tangible success), and the extra breathing space was theirs.

In 2001, Mark E Smith celebrated his 24th year as a member of The Fall. If he completes another twelve months, let's hope someone has the courtesy to buy him a gold clock.

Essential Song: 'Telephone Thing.' Okay, I know it's not The Fall's greatest track (it's not even my favourite number), but this is a book about a certain time and place, and in January 1990 this sounded pretty damn good. It's only disappointing Coldcut didn't push 'Telephone Thing' in the same way as the Yazz-fronted 'The Only Way Is Up.' I mean, can you imagine Mark E Smith closing out *Top Of The Pops* with his trademark scowl? Yes, it's hard but give it a go. See, cool isn't it?

Essential Album: *Grotesque (After The Gramme)*. The classic Fall line-up (Smith, Phil and Steve Hanley, Marc Riley, Craig Scanlon) construct the classic Fall album. Released a decade before baggy, it's so futuristic you'd assume that it was recorded sometime next Tuesday. And if you were still in any doubt that Mark Smith could be a bit of a softy, check out what he told *Q* about the subsequent sacking of Scanlon: "It was a bad decision. And he hasn't picked up a guitar since. I still see him actually, knocking about in Manchester. I do miss him."

The Smiths

Formed 1982. Disbanded 1987.

Key Personnel: Morrissey (vocals), Johnny Marr (guitar), Andy Rourke (bass), Mike Joyce (drums).

When awkward, bespectacled, Dublin-born Steven Patrick Morrissey went up to Tony Wilson and told him he was going to be famous, it was all the Factory boss could do to keep a straight face. Wilson: "I didn't think Steven would be able to keep away from his bedroom long enough to become a success." Paul Morley was also pretty taken aback by Morrissey's ambition: "It's hard to think of anyone who lacked the equipment to succeed in show business quite so badly as Steven when he started out."

What Morley and Wilson didn't know was that the young Steven had devised a plan to secure him a place amongst the stars. At its heart was a recipe that involved taking a bit of James Dean (the quiff, the occassionally worn specs and the inhibited manner), a dash of Johnny Ray (the hearing aid) and a pinch of Oscar Wilde (the ready wit and the gladioli). He brought them together in the form of a person who would hereafter always be referred to as Morrissey. In addition to this elaborate reinvention, the would-be singer/songwriter had the good fortune to cross the path of a talented teenage guitarist called Johnny Marr.

Morrissey and Marr formed a band with Andy Rourke and Mike Joyce and called themselves The Smiths. Morrissey: "It was the most common, most English name we could think of." They toured on and off for six months, winning a following and a contract with Rough Trade. They recorded their debut single, 'Hand In Glove.' It flopped. They recorded a second single, 'This Charming Man.' It was stunning and captured the entire music industry's attention. They delivered a show-stopping performance on *Top Of The Pops* then released their eponymous debut album. It went to number two. They released follow-up LPs, *Hatful Of Hollow* and *Meat Is Murder*. The latter went to number one. Rourke was sacked because of his addiction to heroin and replaced by Craig Gannon. Rourke was reinstated but Gannon stayed on with the band for a while. The Smiths released a fourth LP, *The Queen Is Dead*, but only after a six-month delay caused by friction between the band and Rough Trade. The album topped the chart. The Smiths were through with Rough Trade and signed with EMI. Marr and Morrissey started to quarrel. The quarrels turned to fights. Marr turned his back on the group. Morrissey, Rourke and Joyce tried to keep the ship afloat but failed. The Smiths released their final album, *Strangeways Here We Come*. It went to number one. Morrissey recorded as a solo artist, enjoyed a huge success with debut single 'Suedehead,' toured Britain and America, sold out the Hollywood Bowl quicker than any act ever but never became truly enormous. Marr hooked up with Brian Ferry for reasons that were never fully explained, became an affiliate of The The, freelanced for The Pretenders, formed Electronic with New Order's Bernard Sumner and set up his own fashion house. Joyce, meanwhile, sued Morrissey over unpaid royalties and left court with a cheque for £1m.

The Smiths made excellent singles but seldom cracked the top 10. They recorded albums that sold well but not spectacularly. Their shows were always sell-outs, but they seldom played venues the size of Aston Villa Leisure Centre, never mind Wembley Stadium. So why is it that they've had as much music magazine space dedicated to them as bands a thousand times bigger? And why, more pertinently, are they so readily cited as an influence on the baggy brigade when their look (they resembled mildly effeminate teddy boys) and lyrics (a blend of Noel Coward cunning and Alan Sillitoe sulleness) were so out of step with the movement's overriding obsession with having a good time? The most plausible explanation I've found was offered up by Jonathan Kennaugh in *The Rough Guide To Rock*: 'The Smiths' conviction, integrity and unfailing quality control opened the floodgates for bands such as The Stone Roses and Happy Mondays to reach the mainstream, buoyed by the credibility which The Smiths had brought to the independent sector.' The fact that there weren't too many Madchester pretty boys also suggests that Morrissey's eccentricities and inhibitions might have been instrumental in encouraging shy guys who didn't consider themselves attractive to leave their bedsits and play at being pop stars.

'The Smiths,' concludes Kennaugh, 'stood tall. They made a difference. They truly mattered.' I wish I'd written that.

Essential Song: 'This Charming Man.' With a back catalogue that includes 'William, It Was Really Nothing,' 'How Soon Is Now?,' 'The Queen Is Dead,' 'The Boy With A Thorn In His Side,' 'Girlfriend In A Coma' and 'What Difference Does It Make?,' it's a thankless task to select the greatest ever Morrissey/Marr composition. But this is the track that really started things off for The Smiths. And if you can't hear echoes of it in The Stone Roses and Inspiral Carpets' debut LPs, you must be Helen Keller

Essential Album: *The Queen Is Dead*. Astonishingly talented, if surprisingly unsuccessful, when it came to churning out singles, The Smiths made few truly compelling albums (they actually made few proper LPs full stop, the bulk of their output comprising compilations). This, though, would be a standout on any band's CV even if only for the fine and funny 'Frankly Mr Shankly,' the brutal 'Bigmouth Strikes Again' and the jaw-dropping title track, aka Johnny Marr's guitar showcase. Marr: "I was playing the solo in the studio and was really getting into it. When I stopped, I looked over at the window and the band, the producer and the electricians were all stood there looking stunned. I said, 'Was that okay then?' They said it was fine, generally."

4. The Big Two

While it's hard to pin down exactly who was and who wasn't down with Madchester, there's no dispute over the acts that are most commonly associated with the scene: The Stone Roses and Happy Mondays.

The Stone Roses

Formed in 1980 as The Patrol. Became The Stone Roses in 1985. Disbanded 1996.

Key Personnel: Ian Brown (vocals), John Squire (guitar), Gary 'Mani' Mounfield (bass), Alan 'Reni' Wren (drums).

Ideally, a piece on The Stone Roses should concentrate solely on the music; sweet, intoxicating, grab-you-by-the-balls-and-scoop-you-into-heaven music. However, any article that can hope to do justice to this groundbreaking band has to address other matters: dark, dirty words like Zomba, contract dispute, five-year layoffs, Silvertone and stay-gloss emulsion.

According to rumour, Ian Brown first met John Squire in a sandpit at the age of four. It's a nice story but it's probably as apocryphal as the one about The Stone Roses having once been known as English Rose. What is certain is that, in their early teens Ian Brown, karate enthusiast and fan of The Sex Pistols and The Clash, started to pal around with John Squire, introverted loner and lover of The Beach Boys and The Beatles. Although he's been compared with all sorts of guitar legends, Squire wasn't some juvenile genius like Jimmy Page. He didn't even get his first guitar until he turned 15. No sooner had he become accomplished than he set about forming his first band. The Waterfront featured Squire, bass player Gary Mounfield, guitarist Andy Couzens and a singer called Kaiser. Keen to bring in Brown, Squire dissolved the group and formed The Patrol who in time would become The Stone Roses.

The original Roses line-up comprised Brown, Squire, Couzens, bassist Pete Garner and an intuitive drummer known to everyone as Reni. After a name change to The Stone Roses in 1985, Mani replaced Garner in 1987. By this time Couzens had also gone, reducing the group to a classic four piece. The band had been together three years and had accomplished little except a loyal live following. But if they weren't getting anywhere fast, The Roses were at least honing a distinctive sound. Almost a punk band at the outset, their formative years saw them mesh together all sorts of influences. Writing in *Uncut* magazine, Creation boss Alan McGee argued that The Roses sound was shaped by The Jesus & Mary Chain, a little-known American band called The Three O'Clock and Creation's pride and joy Primal Scream (for years, pundits would argue that The Roses' 'Made Of Stone' was a rip-off of the Scream's 'Velocity Girl'). But there were many other influences (The Byrds, The Adverts, Johnny Thunders, The New York Dolls, George Clinton, *Planet Of The Apes* etc.). So many, in fact, that it was impossible to pin the band's music down. But then perhaps this was part of The Roses' genius.

With the music press taking no interest in them, and their output to date consisting of 'So Young,' which was produced by Martin Hannett but went absolutely nowhere, there was a danger The Roses would wilt before anyone got a chance to hear the wonderful noises they were making. Things changed after they got a manager, club owner Gareth Evans, who found the band free rehearsal space and a record deal with Andy Lauder's Silvertone Records. Evans also arranged for the band to work with New Order's Peter Hook who'd liked the group's second single 'Sally Cinnamon,' another flop, and was keen to try out his producing trousers. The single Hook oversaw, 'Elephant Stone,' did a lot to push The Roses in the direction of stardom. It also revealed that while there was a classic, nay epic, element to their music, The Stone Roses weren't a po-faced proto Led Zeppelin. The B-side, 'Full Fathom Five,' is, to all intents and purposes, 'Elephant Stone' played backwards.

By now, The Roses' ascent had become unstoppable. Despite the fact the music press still would not give them any exposure, their fan base had continued to grow and their gigs had become bigger and bigger. A particularly huge date at Alexandra Palace announced the group as a true national phenomenon. What happened a week later, however, threatened to make The Stone Roses a laughing stock.

"Last week a relatively unknown band sold out London's 7,000 capacity Alexander Palace," so spoke *Late Show* host Tracey McCleod as she prepared to introduce the nation's intelligentsia to The Stone Roses. Up until this point, the band had refused to accommodate the London crowd. "It was a secret Manc thing," Mani remembers, "and we made the industry and everyone in it jump through our hoops. We never came down and went: 'can I suck your cock and get a record deal, please.' Anyway, in the end we thought we'd go on a highbrow BBC2 programme and play our music." Deciding to perform live, the group had no sooner reached the first chorus of 'Made Of Stone' than something disastrous happened. Mani: "We cranked up the guitars and blew all the fuses. The needles must have gone straight into the red and they didn't know how to handle that." The fact things had ground to a sudden halt was actually no bad thing given the poor quality of the performance: the band seemed to be playing at 33rpm and Brown sounded like a goose farting in the fog. What's more, the aborted turn garnered far more press than a fine completed one ever could, particularly as Brown, whose immediate reaction to the power cut was to whine "we're wasting our time, lads," repeatedly bellowed "Amateurs!" as McLeod tried to introduce the next item. Mani: "And even after it all blew up, they said to us, 'Would you mind sticking round to the end, I'm sure we can sort everything out.' We were like 'bugger that' and so off we went."

In the end, it was left to *Top Of The Pops* to do what *The Late Show* could have done: make The Stone Roses the nation's property. The song they performed that night, 'Fools Gold,' was an astonishing slab of funk but it was noticeably absent from the band's eponymous debut long-player. It says a lot about the album, however, that you could leave a song like this off it and in no way harm the record.

The first thing that catches your attention about *The Stone Roses* the LP is its cover. Closely resembling the artwork of American 'action painter' Jackson Pollock, the sleeve was designed, as was virtually all the band's cover art, by John Squire. Asked about the design in *Q* magazine's survey of the '100 Greatest Record Covers Of All Time,' Squire said that he'd got the idea after he and Brown watched a documentary about the 1968 Paris Riots. Entitled 'Bye Bye Badman,' Squire claimed that his work was further inspired by the sea at the Giant's Causeway, The Clash (who were big Pollock fans) and the surreal blue and orange lino that his parents had laid in their bathroom. And while the lemons on the cover were meant to symbolise the fact that the Paris rioters had used the fruit to counteract the police's tear gas, no band that sports citrus fruit on its sleeve was ever in danger of taking itself too seriously. Squire: "I bought a lot of lemons - we had a big budget!"

Inside this classic cover was a truly classic LP. From the opening bars of 'I Wanna Be Adored,' a song less about demanding affection than about deserving success, to the astonishing jam that closes out 'I Am The Resurrection,' it was obvious from the first listen that *The Stone Roses*

45

was no ordinary LP. Not that the band had fallen into the trap of making a legendary album. If that had been the case, you certainly wouldn't have had a song like 'Elizabeth My Dear,' a brief, bitter-sweet reworking of Simon & Garfunkel's 'Scarborough Fair,' appearing at the halfway point. Nor for that matter would The Roses have repeated the trick of playing a track backwards (the sublime 'Don't Stop' is what you get when you reverse the even more sublime 'Waterfall') if they'd been openly aspiring to greatness.

That the record is a truly majestic work has a lot to do with its producer. John Leckie is now a big name in the world of record production, thanks to his work with Radiohead. Back in 1989, however, he was as keen to make a name for himself as The Roses: "Geoff Travis at Rough Trade [with whom the band had nearly signed] sent me a tape with 'She Bangs The Drums,' 'Elephant Stone' and 'I Wanna Be Adored' and I said: 'Yes, yes, yes, I'll do it!' All four of them were pretty special. You had a great drummer, a great guitarist who was pulling up all sorts of sounds, you had a great singer with great words and Mani was a brilliant bass player. The chemistry was right with the four of them, so that's what I got off on. There was a great feeling of positivity about it all, that we were going to make the greatest record ever which is what I always say when I go in with the bands. And here I was with a band and all of them really believed that."

Not even the world's best producer can hit his straps if he's got nothing to work with. Leckie, however, was refining the finest pop gems. The reason records like *The Stone Roses* don't happen very often is because they depend on everyone being at the top of their game. In the case of this album, though, the band weren't just on the ball, they were on a different planet. To find a better rhythm section than Reni and Mani you'd certainly have to look away from these shores. And as for the songwriting of Brown and Squire, trust me - if Lennon & McCartney had written this LP people wouldn't be talking about *Sergeant Pepper's Lonely Hearts Club Band* and *Revolver* in quite the same way.

That *The Stone Roses* finished second to *Sergeant Pepper's Lonely Hearts Club Band* in Channel 4's *Music Of The Millennium* poll appalled Bob Geldof. But The Roses, themselves, were the first to admit their record had feathers. Indeed, Mani is on record as saying he actually doesn't think too much of the album: "It ended up sounding like Herman's

Hermits or something." See what I mean about artists not being the best judges of their own work?

'She Bangs The Drums' and 'Made Of Stone' were released as singles, but they felt like afterthoughts and they certainly weren't needed to improve album sales. No, *The Stone Roses*, with its passionate, confident declaration of intent ('Kiss me where the sun don't shine,' Brown proclaims midway through 'She Bangs The Drums,' 'the past was yours but the future's mine.') was the record that had put the band on top of the Madchester pile. Not that Ian Brown had any doubts that that's where The Roses belonged: "Inspiral Carpets were rubbish. The Charlatans were rubbish. Their manager came and said: 'We've found this kid, he's like a young version of you.' I've never gone on stage and thought I was someone else but The Charlatans have." And if he didn't care much for his rivals, Brown had even less time for the term Madchester: "We didn't want to be associated with Madchester because it was a moneymaking thing and we didn't believe in it."

The seal on The Stone Roses' hugeness took the form of the Spike Island one-day festival, which can perhaps be written off as a brave experiment badly executed. Intent on enjoying their hard-won success, the band set about having a good time, all the time. At least, that's what the papers said. The stories of excess were to come as quite a shock to John Leckie, as he told Radio One: "All the publicity came out - these drunken, drug-taking hooligans, sex-mad, drug-mad, drink-mad - but they weren't. They didn't drink. I'd drink more beer than them." The group did dabble in narcotics, as Brown confessed to *Uncut*: "When we were young, we took speed and then about 1986 we started smoking weed. In 1988, we started taking Es." Not surprisingly these chemical influences had found their way onto the debut album in the form of 'Sugar Spun Sister' (where a list of psychedelic occurrences are equated with the proverbial cows coming home) and 'Waterfall,' the blissed-out story of a girl on acid sailing to France on a cross-Channel ferry. The tales of wretched excess were for the most part, though, the handiwork of manager Gareth Evans, a man whose contribution to The Roses seemed to be becoming increasingly negative.

It was Evans who'd negotiated The Roses' deal with Silvertone/Zomba, a weird affair that meant the group didn't make money from CD sales. Since 90% of the band's music sold on CD and Evans had agreed an eight-album deal with Andy Lauder's label, it was obvious things had to change or they'd be heading for the poorhouse - a circumstance made more ironic by Brown's penchant for parading around in a T-shirt with a string of banknotes embroidered around the collar. Following the release of one last single, the underdeveloped 'One Love,' the band entered one of the most infamous legal fights in music history. Besides sacking Evans, who unsuccessfully sued the band, The Roses sought to free themselves from their Silvertone contract. Label boss Andy Lauder responded by taking out a court injunction against the group, which prevented them from releasing any new material. The Roses might have had messier legal battles (when Music For Nations released some of their early work, the band let their emulsions run away with them and set about the label owner's car with pots of paint) but the music industry had seen little to rival this two-year legal struggle. As the band waited for the case to come to court, they fielded approaches from a number of major labels. Silvertone, meanwhile, used the lengthy proceedings to milk the outgoing act for all they could, releasing unsanctioned singles ('I Wanna Be Adored,' 'Waterfall' and 'I Am The Resurrection' were all culled to the consternation of the band), a remix of 'Fools Gold,' an odd-and-sods compilation called *Turns Into Stone*, a greatest hits album *The Complete Stone Roses*, and a collection of material swept up off the studio floor entitled *Garage Flowers*. Eventually, in March 1991, the band had the first of many days in court and two months later, they were free to sign with Geffen Records.

Legal wrangling alone could not account for the fact that it wasn't until 1994 that the band released another track. Infighting, the enemy of so many bands, had started to afflict The Roses soon after the release of the first album. According to Mani, a big part of the problem was that the group had stopped socialising with one another. John Squire even went so far as to relocate to the Lake District. The fact that the guitarist was beginning to get ideas above his station didn't help matters either, even if it was easy to understand how music paper articles entitled 'The Unforgettable Squire' could have gone to his head. Squire's desire to run the show his way became particularly apparent during the 12 months it took the band to record their follow-up LP. Holed up in North Wales, the guitarist was particularly harsh on Reni, commonly believed to be the most talented musician in the group, and insisted that the band perform over recorded tape loops rather than live drumming. Not only did this destroy the drummer's confidence but it really got up Brown's nose who began to refer to the group as The John Squire Experience. Recalled to the fold, producer John Leckie wasn't too impressed either: "The spark had gone. We knew each other so well and things weren't changing. It's like a love affair. I said: 'If nothing's gonna change, then I'm going.'"

Eventually an album did get made and inevitably it came in for a right kicking. A fabulous first LP and a five-year lay-off meant the weight of expectation was crushing. This being the case, the decision to call the record *Second Coming* wasn't perhaps the most sensible of ideas. The title wasn't half as troublesome as some of the Zeppelin-inspired drivel that The Roses had concocted. Just what had gone wrong? John Squire had no doubts. "There were too many drugs in the studio," he told *The Face*. "The band members were on different drugs at the same time. It can be destructive if everybody's on a different plane." In Squire's case, the problem was cocaine, which he claimed he had become addicted to. Brown, meanwhile, was smoking copious amounts of marijuana and Reni was alleged to be doing something stronger than Rennies. And as for Mani? Well, as Ian Brown explained: "Mani was on everything!"

Drugs weren't the only reason for the sloppiness and self-involvement of *Second Coming* but they might explain its inconsistency. The single 'Ten Storey Love Song' and tracks like 'How Do You Sleep?' had nothing to apologise for and wouldn't have looked at all out of place on *The Stone Roses*. But when Primal Scream's Bobby Gillespie called 'Love Spreads' the greatest comeback single of all time, the question had to be what had *he* been taking? Stodgy and stolid, the track epitomises all that's wrong with the record, although it's worth noting that the version on *Second Coming* is a considerable improvement on the live rendition the band 'contributed' to the *Help* LP.

As the press tore *Second Coming* apart like a pack of dogs, The Roses set about themselves with a sledgehammer. The first to walk was Reni, who left on the eve of the comeback tour for reasons that have never fully been explained. Next to get off the boat was Squire whose leaving in April 1996 should have brought proceedings to a halt. Either through ignorance or arrogance, Brown and Mani soldiered on, recruiting new drummer Robbie Maddix, guitarist Aziz and keyboard player Nigel Ipinson. It was this plucky little band that bowled along to Reading to headline the 1996 festival. Unfortunately, Brown forgot to go to bed the night before and wound up turning in arguably the worst performance of his career. A few months later, a press statement was issued: 'Having spent the last 10 years in the filthiest business in the universe it's a pleasure to announce the end of The Stone Roses. May God bless all who gave us their love and supported us throughout this time, special thanks to the people of Manchester who sent us on our way. Peace be upon you. - Ian Brown, Manchester, 29 October 1996'

"We underachieved somewhat" is how Mani sums up The Stone Roses experience. Certainly, there are limits to what the group accomplished. They didn't break America. They didn't make it beyond the 'difficult' second album. But is it really right to talk about failure when you have Liam Gallagher stealing Ian Brown's act lock, stock and two smoking barrels while you've his brother Noel saying: "The Roses opened the door and then we came along and nailed it to the wall"? Should you really think of yourself as underachievers when your debut album sold 500,000 copies, stayed on chart for almost two years and is regularly called the best LP of the 1980s? And can you really talk about not making it when you have a sound that's been pinched by everyone from The Bluetones to Blur to Cast to The Charlatans? I don't think so.

What happened in the aftermath of The Roses' death was a mixture of the inevitable and the truly surprising. While it was no great shock that Mani's services were in high demand, it was amazing that no one seemed to want to employ Reni's tight-as-a-biscuit tin drum sound. And as it was inevitable that John Squire would continue to make music (and even more inevitable that his act, The Seahorses, would become mired in muso masturbation and longueurs), no one could have predicted what lay in store for Ian Brown. King Monkey had always talked a good game ("We were bigger and better than Led Zeppelin" he once told *Uncut*) so it was no surprise that he predicted solo success but his musicianship was limited and he was never going to win an Eisteddfod with his singing voice.

All of which made his solo debut *Unfinished Monkey Business* such an unexpected delight. To his credit, Brown had worked hard since The Roses split up. He hadn't done anything to improve his voice which was still gloriously untrained, but he'd spent time at the mixing desk and added bass, acoustic guitar, drum and keyboard skills to his songwriting talents. Admittedly, while it wore its reggae influences effectively, *Unfinished Monkey Business* wasn't anything to go ape about. However, it featured three fine singles, 'My Star,' 'Corpses' and 'You Can't See Me,' a blistering attack on John Squire entitled 'Ice Cold Cube' (Reni's nickname for the guitarist) and evidence galore that, if Brown's lyrics hadn't lost their naïveté, he still had a special way with bite and bile. His targets included misplaced patriotism ('Lions'), NASA's profligacy ('My Star') and coke whores ('Corpses'). The LP's charm, meanwhile, sprang from the fact that while, with The Seahorses, Squire had completely turned his back on his Roses past, Brown was keen, if not determined, to collaborate with his former bandmates, hence the presence of Roses' vibe master Cressa, Reading stalwart Aziz and Reni and Mani on 'You Can't See Me,' a sort of mellowed-out companion to 'Fools Gold.' Equally as admirable was the way the singer/songwriter brokered the LP. Out of contract at the time of recording, he simply went into the studio, laid down the tracks and then sold the record directly to Polydor.

Before he was able to capitalise on the qualified success of his solo debut, Brown had to spend some time at Her Majesty's pleasure. Sent down for threatening to chop a flight attendant's hands off, Brown re-emerged from Strangeways four months later, claiming: "I had little respect for authority when I went it, I have no respect for it now." The unscheduled holiday could not interfere with Brown's return to high estate. Indeed, his next release was right up there with his very best work. 'Be There' had begun life as the instrumental 'Unreal' on *Psyence Fiction*, an LP recorded by UNKLE, an experimental act comprising hip hop legend DJ Shadow and Mo Wax head honcho James Lavelle. The addition of Brown's baleful lyrics and ghoulish vocal to the harsh machine sound of the original made for utterly compelling listening.

It was also hard to ignore Brown's second album. Entitled *Golden Greats*, a title presumably chosen with tongue firmly in cheek, it developed the ideas that *Unfinished Monkey Business* had set out. It garnered Brown further hit singles, 'If Dolphins Were Monkeys' and 'Love Like A Fountain,' and his first Brit Award nomination (at 35, he was actually younger than the four other gents nominated for best British Male Artist). Now a happily married family man, Brown has just released LP number three, *Music Of The Spheres*. The verdict? It rocks.

From young Turk to loving husband, Ian Brown has come a hell of a long way. That he hasn't lost his songwriting talent, his ear for music or his sense of humour (his live act features a killer version of Michael Jackson's 'Billie Jean') says much for him. Even if he had become a wash-out rather than a wise man, Brown would still deserve reverence. With his astonishing looks and lyrical gifts, it's hard to think of Brown as an ordinary bloke but you only need to hear his voice to see that here is a man not so far removed from the crowd. Indeed, if you consider that it took The Roses a long time to get a break, that their creative life was relatively short and that the years since have brought mixed fortunes, you can even see him as something of an underdog. Brown, however, has overcome all of the obstacles life has thrown at him. And it's this ability to keep coming back for more, to come out on top despite having the odds so completely weighted against him, that makes Ian Brown the man most spiritually in touch with the North-West experience of the late 1980s and early 1990s. Shaun Ryder might be baggy's clown prince but it's Ian Brown, the loser who won, the dead-end kid who used what he had to escape the cul-de-sac, who is the crown prince of Madchester. Long may he reign.

Essential Song: 'Fools Gold.' One half of what was possibly the best double A-side since 'Penny Lane'/'Strawberry Fields Forever' (it was backed up by the brilliant 'What The World Is Waiting For'), this isn't typical of The Roses' sound but you won't find a better funk work this side of the Atlantic. Reworked and re-released countless times, accept no substitute. Forget the rest, the original's the best.

Essential Album: *The Stone Roses*. Naturally.

Happy Mondays

Formed 1984.

Key Personnel: Shaun Ryder (vocals), Paul Ryder (bass), Mark 'Moose' Day (guitar), Paul 'PD' Davis (keyboards), Gary 'Gaz' Whelan (drums), Mark 'Bez' Berry (Bez).

Right, so you've these six blokes from Manchester. They're all drug dealers, two of them work for the Post Office and one of them is a policeman's son who's been in trouble with the law since the day he was born. Oh, and they want to be rock stars. This isn't a joke.

Everything about the Happy Mondays story is fantastic. New Order have been said to be the beneficiaries of good fortune but if that's the case, then the Mondays are protected from on high by the Prince Of Darkness. Apparently choosing a career in pop because they'd run out of other ways to get high, the band went from nowhere to everywhere, and along the way they committed every sin known to God and quite a few that the good Lord hadn't even thought of. That they ended up back where they started wasn't the point - that they left there in the first place is what makes the Happy Mondays' story both unlikely and curiously loveable.

It all began in the back streets of Manchester, or to be precise 53 Conniston Avenue, Little Hulton, which was where the Ryder brothers Paul and Shaun grew up. By the time he'd turned 18 Shaun had left school without any qualifications, got married to a woman two years older (it wouldn't last), been hired and fired by the Post Office, and embarked on a career as a drug dealer with the assistance of elder brother Paul. It was in this nefarious capacity that the young outlaws ran into Gaz Whelan (a one-time apprentice with Everton Football Club), Mark Day and Whelan's mate Paul Davis. A while later they would encounter Mark Berry, a lad who didn't let being a police officer's son get in the way of having a good time - he was known to everyone as Bez.

At what point these hooligans decided to make music together isn't clear but by 1980, the Happy Mondays were bashing out Joy Division covers. By 1984, they'd graduated to gigging, although they seldom played anywhere more ambitious than a youth club. Their time away from music was spent partying at the Hacienda and selling drugs to the clientele. Come 1985, the group were performing concerts at the night spot and Bez had been hired full time as a dancer cum 'vibe master.' Strange days were on the horizon.

The Mondays' big break came in the shape of a 'battle of the bands' contest. That the group won came as no surprise to them as organiser Tony Wilson told them they had it in the bag before they hit the stage. Signed to Factory, the group commenced work on their formidably titled debut LP *Squirrel & G-Man 24 Hour Party People Plastic Face Carnt Smile (White Out)*. A moniker that would provide the name for both a film and a phenomenon (and which referenced Bez's lawman father), the album was overseen, not by New Order's Bernard Sumner who'd produced a couple of early Mondays recordings, but by The Velvet Underground's John Cale. It was an interesting choice given that the band were heavy drug users and Cale was a former heroin addict. As Dave Simpson noted in his excellent *Uncut* profile of the group, Cale had his sensible hat on and attacked the band over their use of recreational substances. Shaun Ryder, whose drug of choice at the time was marijuana, responded by experimenting with smack.

Ryder Jnr.'s 'new direction' didn't interfere with his creative processes. Indeed, although the album was very loose musically, the songwriting was incredibly sharp. Ryder's lyrical talents had long been evident to Factory's Tony Wilson: "The Mondays wrote a song called 'Tart Tart' and the first verse of 'Tart Tart' is a ten-line encapsulation of Martin Hannett. It describes him completely, it's like a short story, a poem. I suddenly realised one year that Shaun hadn't met Martin Hannett at that point in history. I said to their manager Phil Saxe: 'How did Shaun write so completely, this sketch of Hannett?' He said: 'He used to hang out with Barney Sumner at Dry and Barney would tell him the old stories.' And Shaun could take Barney's stories and turn it into one of the most wonderful pieces of literature." Together with 'Kuff Dam' and '24 Hour Party People,' 'Tart Tart' formed the sweet centre of an LP which was too sloppy for its own good but which suggested that great times were to come.

Not inappropriately, Wilson next insisted that the band hook up with Hannett (also a victim of heroin abuse, incidentally). The veteran's firmish hand and the group's first taste of Ecstasy were crucial in coaxing a remarkable album out of Ryder and the boys. *Bummed* still featured some of *Squirrel & G-Man*'s ragged edges but it was a slicker, more rounded affair. A veritable A to Z of the slut 'n' scumbag lifestyle, tracks like 'Fat Lady Wrestlers' and 'Do It Better' hinted at a saucy, gaudy world previously only glimpsed in the paintings of Beryl Cook and the racy working-class fiction of Alan Sillitoe. 'Lazyitis,' on the other hand, summed up a traditional response to the mundane while simultaneously successfully raiding The Beatles' songbook (a crime that had landed the band in trouble before - *Squirrel & G-Man*'s 'Desmond' bore such a strong resemblance to 'Ob-La-Di, Ob-La-Da' the record had to be recalled and the track removed). The tour de force, however, was 'Mad Cyril,' a track which painted a vivid picture of gangster tripping while doffing its cap to the influence of Big Audio Dynamite (like BAD's 'E=MC$_2$,' 'Mad Cyril' featured samples from Nic Roeg and Donald Cammell's hard men 'n' hard drugs odyssey *Performance*, which was also the title of a song on *Bummed*). Rounding out the LP's scuzzy feel with a centre spread lifted from *Penthouse*'s Readers' Wives strand, the Mondays projected a sound and an image that was anything but embraceable. The appeal to middle-class school kids was obvious, however. On *Bummed*, you had hoodlums singing about a lifestyle that was foreign, exciting and, since you lived in the Home Counties, utterly unthreatening. Like books on The Kray Twins, the Mondays provided access to a sordid, seductive world without subjecting you to the danger that might engulf you if you entered that world for real. Of course, unlike the books, you could groove to the Happy Mondays.

You could groove to them a darn sight easier after Erasure's Vince Clarke got hold of *Bummed*'s 'Wrote For Luck' and reworked it as the shiny, ultra-danceable 'WFL.' Amazed at the magic Clarke had wrought,

Tony Wilson set about teaming the Mondays with DJ duo Paul Oakenfold and Steve Osborne. The first fruit of this collaboration, the 'Madchester Rave On' EP (Wilson came up with the title) brought the band their first top-20 success. It was obvious what the Mondays now had to do… They re-recorded 'He's Gonna Step On You Again' by South Africa's John Kongos which had been a hit over 15 years ago, renamed it 'Step On,' donated it to a compilation album commemorating the anniversary of their American record label Elektra and then kept it for themselves because of its obvious commercial appeal. (To appease Elektra, they recorded another Kongos hit, 'Tokoloshe Man,' for the anniversary LP.) A top-5 hit, 'Step On,' paved the way for 'Kinky Afro,' a reworking of Patti La Belle's 'Lady Marmalade' complete with lyrics about shagging around and graffiti artists, and 'Loose Fit,' a paean to Madchester's dress code that would have charted higher had it not been for the small matter of the Gulf War. For reasons that aren't entirely obvious, the radio authorities took a dim view of the line: 'Gonna buy an air force base/gonna wipe out your race.' The Oakenfold/Osborne wizardry wasn't just restricted to singles, though. Reaching number 4 on the UK album survey, *Pills 'N' Thrills & Bellyaches* was one of the triumphs of the year and tracks like the slutty but extremely sexy 'Bob's Your Uncle,' the dazzling 'Donovan' (an appropriate choice of title since Shaun would shack up with both the hippy legend's twin daughters) and the police baiting 'God's Cop' were a match for anything released in 1990.

After a decade of bumming around, the Mondays had finally made it. Rather admirably, the sudden onset of fame in no way encouraged the group to start behaving like good, responsible citizens. Rather, they carried on like a bunch of louts who'd just won the National Lottery. In Spain to shoot the video for 'Step On,' Shaun skived off for an afternoon of sunbathing and came back so lobster red that the band had to cancel a concert. Bez had helpfully suggested that Shaun treat his sunburn by wrapping himself in bandages and then ripping them off very quickly to remove the damaged skin. Curious that you never saw Bez on *The Krypton Factor*. In Brazil for the Rock In Rio festival, they mimicked their heroes The Sex Pistols by putting on policemen's helmets and arsing about with great train robber Ronnie Biggs. Approached by Malcolm McLaren to contribute to his Channel 4 extravaganza *The Ghost Of Oxford Street*, the group dressed up as highwaymen and sung 'You've Got To Pick A Pocket Or Two' from Lionel Bart's *Oliver!* as they made their way to the gallows.

And when an offer came in from *Penthouse* for Bez and Shaun to pose with nude models in a jacuzzi, well, do you think they needed asking twice?

The fact the Mondays did as they pleased when they pleased could occasionally lead to controversy and Factory had a particularly difficult time defending Bez's homophobic comments. The open courting of chaos also made for some pretty erratic live performances. According to one possibly apocryphal story, Shaun and Bez once rushed from Manchester's Piccadilly Station to a local venue, got there as the opening bars of the first song started to play, dashed on stage... only to find that they were sharing it with Simply Red's Mick Hucknall (the Mondays were playing across town that evening). As this writer can testify, the unplanned feel of a Mondays concert didn't necessarily undermine the quality of the performance. On the contrary, the fact that you had Gaz drumming in complete darkness, Day playing with his back to the audience and Bez doing whatever he wanted gave the gigs such a gloriously improvised feel that you'd think for all the world that you were the first people ever to hear the songs. And while at the NEC in April 1989 there weren't too many people on their feet (they were, after all, only the support act), the group could make a crowd writhe like few other acts. But don't just take my word for it - you can discover for yourself what a delight the Happy Mondays in concert could be by checking out the unimaginatively titled *Live!* recorded at Leeds' Elland Road.

Having been on a high for almost the whole of 1990, it was inevitable that the Mondays would experience some sort of comedown. No one, though, could have predicted the horrific events that lay in store. Delighted with the critical and financial success of *Pills 'N' Thrills & Bellyaches*, Factory packed the group off to the Barbados where they were to record the follow-up with Tina Weymouth and Chris Frantz of Talking Heads and Tom Tom Club fame. Wilson had twice tempted fate before by having the band work with producers who'd come a cropper on the narcotics front. But to send Shaun Ryder to the Caribbean just as a blizzard of cocaine was starting to settle was asking for trouble once too often. With crack trading on the island for a dollar a rock, it wasn't long before Ryder was on the road to serious addiction. Weeks of studio time were eaten up as Shaun patrolled the island in pursuit of drugs. Eventually, Frantz got hold of Ryder, locked him in his hotel room and told him not to come out until he'd written some lyrics. Shaun's response? To break out of the window and then go and sell his clothes for cocaine. When he eventually returned to Britain, the singer/songwriter claimed that he was devouring thirteen rocks of crack a day, enough to leave him incapacitated (although as David Baddiel observed: "I'd be incapacitated if I ate thirteen Curly-Wurlys a day."). Compared to Shaun's bingeing, Bez breaking his arm and then getting the wound so severely infected he almost required amputation was a mere inconvenience.

Anthony Wilson remembers that the mayhem surrounding the making of the LP that became ...*Yes Please* continued right up until the end of recording: "On the night we pulled the plugs, just at the very last minute, we managed to find that Shaun had opened the back fire doors of Eddy Grant's studio and was shifting the two studio sofas into a van to take down to town to sell for crack." Wilson also recalls walking along the ocean front and seeing local drug dealer Bobby The Diver strolling past him wearing Wilson's Armani jacket and trousers. Wilson: "I wonder how he got them?"

That the LP was finished at all was quite a feat. Musically, however, it couldn't have been shorter of ideas. And as for Ryder's lyrics, it was obvious he had other matters on his mind. What's more, the record had cost over £250,000 to record, a sum that sent the already financially rocky Factory even further into the red ...*Yes Please*? No thank you, more like.

Reaching number 14 on the UK album chart, ...*Yes Please* would have been considered a triumph by many Indie bands. Once you take into account the Mondays' previous successes and the massive expense, you appreciate why the record effectively spelt the end of the band. While Ryder went off into rehab (his crack habit having been supplanted by acute heroin addiction), the Mondays talked about continuing with backing singer Rowetta taking over on lead vocals ("She's Shaun with tits," reasoned Bez) and keyboardist Paul Davis writing the songs. One listen to Paul Davis' demos was enough to put the mockers on that. By 1993, Happy Mondays were no more.

That it took 11 years to break up the Happy Mondays is incredible when you consider it could just as easily have taken 11 minutes. And as for what they achieved in their time together, it was more telling than that accomplished by many groups with considerably more talent. In his *Uncut* piece, Dave Simpson reasons that the Mondays' music and their DJ collaborations inspired everything from U2's *Achtung Baby* and The Prodigy's 'Firestarter' to Blur's hooking up with William Orbit and Suede aligning themselves with Steve Osborne. The group's cultural impact, on the other hand, has been so great that, nine years on from their heyday, Sky Sports' *Soccer AM*, possibly the greatest television show of all time, features a soccer memorabilia and merchandise skit in which the items in question are brought on by a 'Stereotypical resident of Manchester' monkey dancing to 'Step On.'

What's really strange about the Happy Mondays' story, though, is that the breaking of the band and the ravaging of Shaun Ryder wasn't the end of the story. Indeed, in Ryder's case at least, the best was still to come. After two years in the wilderness, no one was exactly holding their breath when Ryder Jnr. announced his return to rock with Black Grape, an outfit featuring himself, Bez, drummer Ged Lynch, guitarist Paul 'Wags' Wagstaff and Paul 'Kermit' Leveridge, formerly of cult favourites The Ruthless Rap Assassins. As Matthew Grant observed in *The Rough Guide To Rock*, Ryder had formed the band in his living room shortly after the Mondays split. It wasn't until 1995, however, that Black Grape unleashed *It's Great When You're Straight... Yeah!*, an astonishing record, jam packed with manic originality, great rhythms and even better rhymes ('Jesus was a black man/No, Jesus was Batman'). Nominated for the Mercury Music Prize, it spawned three top-20 singles, 'Reverend Black Grape' (an exposé of the Catholic Church's dark dealings during World War II whose lines about there being 'nothing more sinister than ministers in dresses' ruffled the feathers at the Papacy), 'Kelly's Heroes' and 'In The Name Of The Father,' and restored Ryder's reputation as a truly important artist.

Taking a little under a year to make it, Black Grape took roughly the same amount of time to fall apart. The collapse was a little surprising as the group had proven that they could recover from failure, the stolid 'Fat Neck' having been immediately followed up by 'England's Irie,' a football anthem featuring guest performances from Keith Allen and Joe Strummer which knocked the FA's official Euro '96 song, Baddiel, Skinner and Brodie's 'Three Lions,' into a cocked hat. However, when the singles 'Get Higher' and 'Marbles' and a second album *Stupid, Stupid, Stupid* all flopped, the band succumbed to squabbling and unceremoniously split up.

What was particularly sad about the end of Black Grape was the fact the band seemed to have got through the bad times. Heck, they'd even made a film about them. *The Grape Tapes* is the sort of hymn to hedonism and disorganisation that most record companies would have gone to great lengths to hush up. Its director, 'Too Nice' Tom Bruggen says of his doc-umentary: "Most of what we shot for the film we couldn't use. A lot of it we'd get arrested for, but it would be good for a wank. It'd go down well with people inside. There's one subliminal shot of someone's genitals [author's note: the someone was comedian and Grape affiliate Keith Allen who got a good telling off for flashing his old chap at host Julia Carling]. It was during the 'England's Irie' *Top Of The Pops* performance. Producer Ric Blaxhill took it out but I was there with my camera. *The News Of The World* offered £15,000 for it. However, Shaun and I don't want to go through our whole lives looking like shitheads and arseholes." More's the pity. The many memorable moments Bruggen captured included Kermit being hospitalised because of drug problems and the band successfully convincing a US police officer, a breed not noted for their leniency, that there isn't sufficient cannabis on the tour bus to make a search worth-while. Unfortunately, a clip of a stoned Shaun Ryder falling asleep during a US radio interview and setting fire to a microphone did not make the final cut.

But even Black Grape going sour didn't spell the end for Shaun Ryder. Demand for the man's music remained so great that, in 1999, he reassem-bled the Mondays to record a cover of Thin Lizzy's 'The Boys Are Back In Town' by way of promoting a superfluous *Greatest Hits* album (the pretty comprehensive *Loads* had been released three years earlier) and to play some festival dates. Admittedly, the decision to put the group back together was entirely financial (the lead singer having received a tax demand rumoured to be in the region of £400,000) but the thousands who braved the Glastonbury quagmire to mimic Bez's freaky dancin' in the midst of a hurricane couldn't have cared less.

The comeback was, alas, short lived. Ryder's behaviour became so erratic that he attacked Rowetta en route to a concert in Ireland, an assault which resulted in both the backing singer and Bez quitting the band. With the Mondays now back on the scrap heap and Ryder in anything but rude health, things look very black indeed. However, you can never write the singer off. The fact that he's still alive makes a mockery of the odds. Another brilliant album is not out of the question.

Essential Song: 'Step On.' If you think about it, this really shouldn't work at all. A stodgy song, clumsy sampled piano, nothing that could be mistaken for singing - it's a recipe for disaster. That it actually works wonderfully says an awful lot about the Mondays but maybe more about

Madchester, a time and place where imperfect planning didn't necessarily result in piss poor performance.

Essential Album: *Pills 'N' Thrills & Bellyaches*. Neither as coherent nor as polished as *The Stone Roses*, this remains one of the most important albums of its time if only because of Ryder's songwriting and the heady mix of high times and low lives that infuses every track.

5. The Also-Bands

The Charlatans

Formed 1989.

Key Personnel: Tim Burgess (vocals), Martin Blunt (bass), Rob Collins (keyboards), Jon Brookes (drums), Jon Baker (guitar), Tony Rogers (keyboards).

The Charlatans were considered a part of the Madchester scene long before anyone realised that most of them actually came from the West Midlands. But as Craig McClean noted in a *Daily Telegraph* profile on the band's Cheshire-born frontman Tim Burgess, the group's distinctly baggy sound was no help at all in landing them a recording contract. In the end, the band's manager Steve Harrison scrapped together enough money to allow the group to print and press their first single, 'Indian Rope,' independently in February 1989. Six months later, their debut album *Some Friendly* was sitting at the top of the UK charts and the single 'The Only One I Know' was being hailed as one of the year's highlights.

Pop stars being pop stars, it didn't take The Charlatans long to piss away their good start. A second album, *Between 10th And 11th*, played like a study in career suicide, the jangly pop of *Some Friendly* having been stripped away and replaced with an experimental sound which, though compelling, was nobody's idea of commercial (the singles the LP spawned, 'Weirdo' and 'Tremelo Song,' were interesting but also failed to shift units). To compound matters, guitarist Jon Baker quit, bass player Martin Blunt was hospitalised with clinical depression and keyboardist Rob Collins found himself serving four months for participating in the armed robbery of a West Midlands off-licence.

It seems that you could have added a typhoon to this avalanche of misfortune and you still couldn't have stopped The Charlatans. A third album, *Up To Our Hips*, saw them return to what they did best and they were rewarded with their seventh top-40 hit, 'I Never Want An Easy Life If Me And He Were Ever To Get There.' It was also around this time that Burgess enjoyed a fruitful relationship with The Chemical Brothers, recording 'Life Is Sweet' for the Brothers' *Exit Planet Dust* album and reworking Sly & The Family Stone's 'Time For Living' to great effect for the *Help* LP. (Burgess has a lot to thank Messrs Rowlands and Simons for - he met his wife at an LA Chemical Brothers concert.)

The Charlatans next long-player could have benefited from some of the Brothers' invention. Indeed, some critics, forgetting their chronology, suggested that when Rob Collins had left prison he must have headed straight down to Our Price and bought up all the recent chart hits as both the band's fourth eponymous album and, in particular, the single 'Just When You're Thinking Things Over' already sounded a bit dated. Not that this seemed to bother the record-buying public who ensured the LP became The Charlatans' second chart topper. Impressive sales could not stem the band's run of bad luck however, and a US tour ran in trouble because of Collins' criminal record. Alas, much, much worse lay in the future. In Wales to record their fifth album, *Tellin' Stories*, The Charlatans had been enjoying a late night drink when Rob Collins decided to drive home. Not wearing a seat belt and well over the legal limit, the keyboardist collided with a hedge and was thrown through the windscreen. He was rushed to Abergaveny Hospital but was pronounced dead soon after his arrival.

Losing a band member must be the worst thing that can ever happen to a group. The way The Charlatans reacted to the loss of Collins is truly inspirational. Originally questioning the relevancy of continuing, the band were convinced to press on by Collins' father and by friends. Primal Scream loaned The Charlatans their keyboardist Martin Duffy so that The Charlatans could fulfil a commitment to support Oasis at their massive Knebworth extravaganza. The group also issued their famous 'We are rock' press release. Pompous yes, but perhaps the very thing they needed to say out loud. It was extraordinary that they found the will to go on in the wake of Collins' death. Even more extraordinary is the music they conjured up. When Dave Grohl founded the Foo Fighters, there was a sudden realisation that for all the pain of losing a bandmate, there is something within music that makes pressing on almost an essential, rather than a reasonable, option. The same can be said of The Charlatans, whose *Tellin' Stories* mourned the passing of their mate but also spawned their finest batch of singles: 'One To Another,' 'North Country Boy' and 'How High.'

After the unqualified triumph of *Tellin' Stories*, it was inevitable that The Charlatans' next release would seem comparatively tame and, sure enough, *Us & Us Only* failed to set the pop world on fire (there was nothing wrong with the single 'Forever,' mind). However, album number seven, *Wonderland*, was a magnificent record and one that dispelled any

doubt that The Charlatans were no longer relevant. As with *Tellin' Sto.*
the record was made in the midst of a tragedy, with Rob Collins' full-time
replacement Tony Rogers discovering that he had testicular cancer. Talking with Craig McClean, Rogers was pretty matter-of-fact about his con-
dition: "My GP told me to just to keep an eye on it, because it didn't seem
to be getting bigger. But five weeks later it had enlarged. The stupid thing
was that I didn't go back to the doctor, because we were in the middle of
the album. I didn't want to disrupt things." Now only one gonad to the
good, Rogers remains confident that he will conquer the illness.

This ability to keep bouncing back, to keep taking things on the chin, to
keep lazy music writers in clichés, is something McLean questioned Tim
Burgess about at length: "Why have we survived? Because we're The
Charlatans. Because initially we didn't get it right. We were stumbling
along doing our thing and people related to it because it was totally hon-
est. But we were learning as we went. The whole band is a unit. Nobody
has to deal with anything on their own, come good things or bad. We do
seem to be the unluckiest band in the world, but I'd turn that round: we're
the luckiest. I think our karma's really good, I do. Are we cursed? No.
And if we are, it's only to teach us a few things."

Depression, imprisonment, death, cancer... The Charlatans have survived it all. Rather like Keith Richards, it would seem they cannot be
killed by conventional weapons. God has blessed the band with immortal-
ity. Which is fine, since he also blessed us with them.

Essential Song: 'The Only One I Know.' The weird introduction, the
swirling organ, Tim Burgess' breathy vocals... a strong contender for the
best single of the Madchester era.

Essential Album: *Tellin' Stories*. An extraordinary record that manages
to mourn the passing of Rob Collins (both on 'How Can You Leave Us'
and 'Rob's Theme,' the latter featuring a clip of Collins as a toddler chat-
ting with his aunt) without becoming maudlin. More cherishable still,
however, is the fact that, in coming to terms with their loss, The Charlatans managed to make a record that helps you realise why you love your
life. If things are going great, stick on 'How High' and take it to the next
level. And if you're feeling low and you'd like to be reminded how important you are, a listen to 'North Country Boy' will confirm your worth.
Even if you come from Kent.

ies.

1983.

sonnel: Tim Booth (vocals), Gavan Whelan (drums), Jim Glen-
___, Paul Gilbertson (guitar), Larry Gott (guitar), David Baynton-
Powell (drums), Saul Davies (violin), Andy Diagram (trumpet), Mark
Hunter (keyboards).

I think it's fair to say that James have never been truly loved. Admired
yes, respected certainly, but something seems to have prevented them
from enjoying the same devotion as many of their contemporaries. Maybe
it's due to Tim Booth's camp cleverness (a man who claims his favourite
word in the English language is fingers, he has said that he'd like his epi-
taph to read 'Nice Try'). Or it could be those bloody awful dresses he used
to wear on tour. Or those flowery 'Come Home' and 'Sit Down' T-shirts
that your loathsome little brother used to flounce about in. Or the fact that
you couldn't walk successfully across a nightclub floor in the 1990s without bumping into some dumbo sat on his ass, bent on a literal interpreta-
tion of the lyrics to the band's most celebrated song (as comedian Ed
Byrne observed: "It would be disastrous if the same thing happened when
you were at a disco with a girl called Eileen and Dexy's Midnight Runners
came on").

If they were hard to adore, it was difficult not to be impressed by
James' resilience. Signed to Factory in 1983, the group went through a
number of record companies and band members before finally making it
in 1989. Success finally came in the form of their debut release for Fon-
tana. A showcase for James' polite Indie pop, *Gold Mother* centred on an
interesting if overproduced collaboration with fellow Mancs Inspiral Carpets ('Mother Gold') and two great singles, 'How Was It For You' and
'Come Home.' Bigger still, but not originally included on the album, was
'Sit Down,' an anthem for the disaffected that reached number 2 in April
1991. Looking back, it's hard to understand why the obvious 'Come
Home' faired better than 'How Was It For You,' a genuinely joyous ode
to post-coital pillow talk. Nevertheless, the audience participation that
contributed to the success of 'Come Home' would come to shape the
band's sound for the worse.

The desire to cash in on *Gold Mother*'s success also didn't do James
too many favours as they were seemingly rushed into the recording of follow-up LP *Seven*. The end result was a big, grandiose record, quite at odds
with the quirkiness and understatement of their earlier work. Singles like

'Sound' and 'Born Of Frustration' smacked of production and vocal excess, Booth having apparently been given a licence to warble over songs in any way he saw fit. To make matters worse, the third single culled from *Seven*, 'Ring The Bells,' was championed by Radio One's Mr 'Our Tune,' Simon Bates.

A decision to hook up with Brian Eno appeared to provide James with a way back to their roots and the resultant *Laid* (1993), though flawed, contained songs that their early incarnation would have been proud of. The title track was a particular delight, although the title, the lyric ('She only comes when she's on top') and the video (featuring Booth dancing around in a dress) stifled sales somewhat. The LP fared a little better, and significant unit shifting in America led to James joining the Lollapalooza tour. Again, the exposure to big crowds seemed to have a negative effect on the group whose next album, *Whiplash*, saw some of the bad habits of *Seven* resurfacing. That said, the LP did feature one fantastic single, 'She's A Star,' and that, together with the fact that for all the ups and downs of the previous years James had somehow managed to rack up 14 hit singles, was enough to convince them to release *James: Best Of...* in 1998. James are not the most confident of bands. Saul Davies told MTV that the group had wanted to call the LP *The Collection* rather than *Best Of* as they didn't consider themselves to have been very successful. New label Mercury persuaded them otherwise.

The album sold well, the way greatest hits albums tend to do. James, however, were now clearly at the crossroads. The success of their next long-player would be crucial to the future of the band. Fortunately, this most unpredictable of acts chose this occasion to produce their finest work to date. From the lushly romantic 'Feel Like Fred Astaire' to the defiant 'I Know What I'm Here For,' *Millionaires* was an album James had long suggested lay within them but had never looked close to delivering. Critically applauded, it also proved that the group didn't need to rely on retrospectives and rehashes of old hits in order to worry the charts.

Unsurprisingly, James haven't been able to keep up this winning form. Their most recent album, 2001's *Pleased To Meet You*, is remarkable only for its cover shot (a clever amalgamation of the band members' faces). However, *Millionaires* granted the band a stay of execution that should see them good for a couple more LP releases and who knows what they could hold in store? And at least they seem to have put the dress thing behind them.

Essential Song: 'Sit Down.' Sure, you could live without ever hearing it again. But if you believe that records can be time machines, then if you ever need a route back to 1991, this is the TARDIS for you.

Essential Album: *Millionaires*. *Gold Mother* was James' Madchester album and it's all well and good. *Millionaires*, however, is not only better, it's a thousand times better. It's a touching example of how not all baggy bands went extinct or became laughing stocks. Some of them actually matured.

Inspiral Carpets

Formed 1987. Disbanded 1994.

Key Personnel: Tom Hingley (vocals), Clint Boon (organ), Martin Walsh (bass), Craig Gill (drums), Graham Lambert (guitars).

The two things that are well known about Oldham's Inspiral Carpets are i) they single-handedly revived interest in the Hammond Organ, an instrument that seemed to have gone the way of the dinosaurs after *Sale Of The Century* went off air and ii) their fans, besides having a penchant for mooing, had a tendency to get arrested, not for ill behaviour or drug offences, but for wearing the band's 'Cool As Fuck' tour T-shirts.

But there's more essential Inspirals trivia that you should familiarise yourself with, such as the fact that their debut independent release, 1988's 'Planecrash' EP, was endorsed by Oldham FC manager Joe Royle. What's also not widely known is that the band went through significant line-up changes before they hit the big time. Besides going through eleven bass players, singer Steve Holt and guitarist Dave Swift departed to make way for Tom Hingley and Martin 'Bungle' Walsh respectively. The band also surrendered the services of strummer Mark Jordan who would go on to play PC Bellamy in ITV's hugely successful Sunday night drama series *Heartbeat*.

The 'big time' for Inspiral Carpets meant their 1990 album *Life*. Wrapped in a silhoutte-laiden sleeve that seemed to poke fun at the Tommy Boy logo, the decidedly Hammond-friendly LP effortlessly blended the sullen 'Sackville,' with the upbeat 'Monkey On My Back' and 'Directing Traffic,' and yielded three hit singles: 'Move,' 'This Is How It Feels' and 'She Comes In The Fall.' If *Life* hitting the number one spot was sign enough of the Inspirals' enormity, the group also found themselves in the strange position of having one of their early releases,

'Find Out Why' reworked as the theme for *The Eight-Fifteen From Manchester*, the summer stand-in for hit children's TV show *Going Live*.

Perhaps it was this incongruity that explained why the band, although keen to quickly follow up their success, also longed for a change in direction. Instead of fully realising the upbeat aspect of their music, the Inspirals moved away from the light. The end result, 1991's *The Beast Inside*, was an abysmal record, overloaded with the sort of dark, navel-gazing you'd more readily associate with Lou Reed, only without the humour. Completely lacking *Life*'s vitality, the record's sales swiftly tailed off and, of the three singles released, only 'Caravan' cracked the top 30.

Having swung too far one way, Inspiral Carpets then overcompensated by swinging a little too far in the other direction. *Revenge Of The Goldfish* (even the title is a little too knowingly upbeat and offhand) certainly featured its share of great tunes, top-20 hit 'Dragging Me Down' being a particular delight, but while critics talked it up as being even better than *Life*, the record-buying public weren't convinced and both the LP and later singles 'Generations' and 'Two Worlds Collide' failed to sell as both the band and their label Mute might have hoped. Fourth album *Devil Hopping* was also a commercial disappointment.

And that, aside from a 'Best Of...' compilation, was that for Inspiral Carpets. As Graham Lambert recently recalled: "We had a lot of creative control in our contract - maybe too much. We ended up a quarter of a million pounds in debt and got dropped by Mute at Christmas '94. The worst thing was trying to keep it from our parents over the Christmas period." Although the band talked to Chrysalis and Nude Records, they were unable to make a deal and decided to split up. Brilliantly monikered organist Clint Boon got married and formed the Clint Boon Experience while also taking on the odd bit of TV work. Lambert took to handling tours by Gomez and Cast. Craig Gill set up a record shop and launched the very fine Proud Mary. And Tom Hingley hit the revival circuit, a drudgery that has subsequently led to him hooking up with Martin Walsh (who had previously busied himself writing music for video games) and saw him support Ian Brown in Manchester in front of 20,000 people on Millennium New Year's Eve.

In the end, it was perhaps inevitable that the Inspiral Carpets' pop escapade would be a short one. So idiosyncratic was their style that there was always the danger that they were going to be considered some sort of novelty. If embracing the organ was a charming if ultimately career-shortening move, there was no denying the sincerity of their songwriting. And while you could sneer at the baggy tops and bowl haircuts, the Inspirals were such an inoffensive lot that it was hard to harbour them any ill will. As Clint Boon summed it up: "When we get to the gates of Heaven we'll get our just rewards. Saint Peter will call us up and say: 'Inspiral Carpets - good songwriters, strong melodies and fine harmonies. Dodgy middle eights, but we'll let you off. In you go.'"

Even if you put their contribution to the British music to one side, a single act alone guaranteed Inspiral Carpets a place in the annals of rock. On 21 November 1988, the band unsuccessfully auditioned a guitarist but decided to keep him on as a roadie. His name was Noel Gallagher. He also had a younger brother.

Essential Song: 'This Is How It Feels.' Proof that in the midst of Madchester's high times, it was possible to write a stark, astonishingly beautiful song about domestic discontent and teen suicide.

Essential Album: *Life*. One of the biggest albums of its era, this now actually sounds quite dated. Not in a bad way, you understand, but in a way that marks it out as perhaps the ultimate Madchester album. It is so clearly the product of a time that has long since passed and a place that has, spiritually at least, ceased to exist.

808 State

Formed 1988.

Key Personnel: Martin Price (keyboards), Graham Massey (keyboards), Gerald Simpson (DJ), Andrew Barker (DJ), Darren Partington (DJ).

It's rather appropriate that 808 State, a band whose career centred on turntables, were formed in a record shop, Martin Price's Eastern Bloc Records to be precise. Impressed with the house music that was then coming out of Detroit and New York, Price gathered up pals Gerald Simpson and Graham Massey (formerly of The Biting Tongues) and got to work.

Naming themselves after a drum machine, the act hit pay dirt almost immediately with 'Pacific State' which grazed the top 10 in December 1989. Recorded almost 18 months earlier, the record had become a big deal on the dance floor before it was decided to foist it upon the mainstream. The release of the single provided Price and Co. with an opportunity to pursue their love of acid house on two long-players, *Newbuild* and

Quadrastate, the latter of which pointed towards the commercial sound that would ensure future single and album success.

It was, alas, at this point that Simpson went his separate way. Keen to keep recording, he became A Guy Called Gerald, a guise beneath which he would create one of the pivotal records of the day, 'Voodoo Ray.' An amazing example of what happens when Detroit Techno is filtered through the Manchester dance scene, it's a measure of the record's might that despite an apparent lack of commercial appeal, nothing could stop it breaking into the top 20. Subsequent releases might not have fared as well commercially, but as far as kudos are concerned, Simpson's stock couldn't be any higher. The only black mark against Simpson's name being the fact that he discovered pot-bellied reggae pretender Finlay Quaye.

Never ones to make it easy for themselves, 808 State chose this juncture to hook up with MC Tunes, a Manchester rapper with a love of pit bull terriers and baseball bats (he was rumoured to be involved in gang activity within the city) and a voice that sounded like he'd been gargling bourbon. It was a peculiar marriage but one that worked for the singles 'Tunes Splits The Atom' (featuring an audacious sampling of The Stone Roses' 'I Am The Resurrection') and 'The Only Rhyme That Bites' (built around the theme from Gregory Peck western *The Big Country*) and the LP *The North At Its Heights*.

Equally successful were the album *Ex:El*, the double A-side 'Cubik'/'Olympic' and 'In Yer Face.' The latter is perhaps the best example of the act's special variety of metal machine music. It is a blend of harsh break beats and slightly discordant rhythms that others would struggle to make work but 808 State pull off easily.

Amazingly, subsequent releases 'Oops' and 'Lift' reached the band's high-quality threshold but charted poorly. But with things starting to turn sour on the recording front, and with Price having left to record as Switzerland, 808 State simply set themselves up as an ace remixing outfit. Besides reworking tracks for Quincy Jones, Primal Scream and, ahem, Rolf Harris, 808 became the first act ever to remix a track for REM. As Andrew Barker recently explained to *Q*: "I'm the REM fan of the band, so I suggested to the other lads: 'Why don't we have a go, see if we can persuade them to let us do a remix?' To our surprise, we got a note from Michael saying if we needed him to do any extra vocals or anything, he'd pop over. Within two weeks of us asking, it was done. They liked it, our fans liked it, everyone was happy."

In addition to their freelance remixing work, 808 State continued to record new material. Their later work featured guest appearances from The Manic Street Preachers' James Dean Bradfield ('Lopez') and their old mate MC Tunes ('Pump Your Fist'). Their most significant recent releases include the retrospective *808:88:98* and *Don Solaris*, an LP that showed that while the jowls were growing and the hair was thinning, 808 State remained way ahead of the game.

Still recording and still a big draw on the dance festival circuit, 808 State have been cited as a key influence by acts like Basement Jaxx and Aphex Twin (who volunteered his services when Massey began remixing *Newbuild* in 1999). And if only because they helped The Prodigy and The Chemical Brothers realise what a few ugly blokes could achieve with some turntables, some synths and a bit of bravado, 808 State's place in pop pantheon should be assured.

Essential Song: 'Pacific State.' Jungle juices combine with the proof that synthesised wind instruments needn't sound naff. This record proves that while making dance records is as easy as assembling Ikea furniture, making good dance records is harder than Chinese maths.

Essential Album: *Ex:El*. The LP that set the trend for the modern dance album. A smattering of guest artists (Bernard Sumner, Bjork, MC Tunes), a couple of killers, a few fillers and a lack of an overall picture. However, if it's a great collection of sounds you're looking for, look no further.

Primal Scream

Formed 1984.

Key Personnel: Bobby Gillespie (vocals), Jim Beattie (guitar), Andrew Innes (guitar), Robert Young (guitar), Martin Duffy (keyboards), Gary 'Mani' Mounfield (bass), Duncan Mackay (horns), Jim Hunt (horns), Darrin Mooney (drums).

To have a West Midlands/North-West act like The Charlatans in a book about the baggy scene is one thing, but to include a band who came together in London and whose lead singer is Glaswegian is quite another. Primal Scream's Madchester credentials are, however, second to none. Not only does ex-Stone Rose Mani now perform with the band but The Stone Roses made no bones about the fact that the Scream's sound influenced their debut LP. What's more, the group contributed greatly to the E

70

culture that emerged in the early 1990s and which was, to begin with at least, largely a North-West phenomenon.

Rather like The Fall, Primal Scream have a band roster that resembles the population of a small country. The one constant has been vocalist Bobby Gillespie, formerly the drummer with East Kilbride's finest, The Jesus & Mary Chain. Signed to Alan McGee's Creation Records, the Scream recorded a few unsuccessful singles before laying down an album, *Sonic Flower Groove*. Both this and follow-up LP *Primal Scream* were pretty interesting fare, but the Stones-influenced rock that was evidenced on these releases gave little indication of the change of direction Primal Scream were about to take.

The change was presaged by a decision to hook up with producer Andrew Weatherall, who promptly got hold of one of the tracks from the *Primal Scream* LP, 'I'm Losing More Than I'll Ever Have,' completely reworked it, slapped on a sampled intro from Richard Rush's Jack Nicholson vehicle *Psych-Out* and marketed the end product as the acid anthem 'Loaded.' Buoyed by the track's top-10 success, Primal Scream created a further batch of equally spaced-out singles, 'Come Together,' 'Higher Than The Sun,' 'Don't Fight It Feel It' and the 'Movin' On Up'-fronted 'Dixie Narco' EP, which were swept together on the album *Screamadelica*. This album was a towering achievement both because of the tracks it contained and due to the band's prodigious drug intake at the time it was recorded. The LP won the inaugural Mercury Music Prize.

While they might have aided the creative process, drugs were to cause Primal Scream their fair share of problems. As *Q* magazine reported, Martin Duffy was out clubbing in New York one time when he suddenly realised that he was bleeding profusely from a stab wound in his backside. Rushed to hospital, Duffy's wound was stitched up and he was sent home, convinced that he'd been slashed in a crowded bar. That was until the following morning when he received a phone call from a friend, demanding that Duffy apologise for falling through his coffee table after unsuccessfully trying to climb up a bookcase. The drugs didn't always work for Bobby Gillespie, either, as anyone who has ever seen that piece of footage where an interviewer asks him to describe his new album will testify. Gillespie's response? To say nothing for a good minute and then mutter "er... I don't know."

Having scaled great heights, Primal Scream lost their way a little. Indeed, it was debatable that their follow-up album *Give Out But Don't*

Give Up was of considerably less interest than an interview Gillespie gave to *Select* magazine in which he asked his co-interviewee, Antipodean pop midget Kylie Minogue, how she felt about the fact so many young men thought about her when they masturbated. The LP itself saw the band rediscovering their infatuation with The Rolling Stones on 'Jailbird' and 'Rocks' (MTV's Beavis & Butthead would ponder what it was that caused a man to sing 'Get your rock salt, get your rock salt, honey'), experimenting with soul on '(I'm Gonna) Cry Myself Blind' and indulging their love of George Clinton's P-funk by having the man himself perform the title track. Loathed by critics at the time, it's now hard to see anything much to hate about the album other than the fact that it clearly isn't a second *Screamadelica*. But then maybe that was the problem.

In typically idiosyncratic style, Gillespie and Co. rehabbed from their critical mauling by joining up with On-U Sound and *Trainspotting* author Irvine Welsh to record the Scottish football team's Euro 1996 song, formidably entitled 'The Big Man And The Scream Team Meet The Barmy Army Up Town.' In equally eccentric fashion, the band then set about making an LP influenced by road movies and the reggae of King Tubby. Indeed, Bobby Gillespie was such as big fan of Richard Sarafin's *Vanishing Point*, a film about an outlaw hero called Kowalski whose flight from the law is assisted by a DJ called Super Soul, that he commandeered the name for the album. "It's a good fuckin' paranoid, speed-freak punk-rock movie," he enthused to *Neon* magazine. "It's a great rock 'n' roll film," he added before explaining why, not content with nicking the name, he also decided to call one of the tracks on the album 'Kowalski': "We did the track because we never thought that the music was that great. We wanted to make music that really suited the film." Since this is a film in which the hero is robbed by gay hitchhikers, loses his girlfriend in a surfing accident and ends up committing suicide by driving his Dodge Charger into a bulldozer, you can imagine that the music the band made was pretty fucked up. The video for 'Kowalski' was also pretty bizarre, featuring as it did Super Model Kate Moss systematically wiping out the members of the band. Gillespie: "How did it feel to be killed by Kate Moss? Amazin'! She karate-chopped me in the neck. She was great - a natural born killer." However, the influences gelled, the tracks worked, the critics were ecstatic and the Scream were nominated for the 1997 Mercury Prize (they eventually lost out to Roni Size).

As *Vanishing Point* set them back on the road to hugeness, so Primal Scream's most recent release resulted in their being recognised once again as one of the nation's most important bands. The last album to be released on Creation Records, *Xtrmntr* was, to put it bluntly, fckn xcllnt. As for what happens next, well, they say rock 'n' roll is a young man's game and both Bobby Gillespie and Mani are now 37. Thankfully, neither show any signs of giving out or giving up.

Essential Song: 'Loaded.' Yes, it sounds like a slowed-down version of 'Sympathy For The Devil.' Yes, it begins with a quote from a ridiculously obscure film. Yes, it's unbelievably cool. Yes, it goes on for bloody ages. And yes, it is always over too quickly.

Essential Album: *Screamadelica*. Drugs were consumed during the making of this album. As to whether it sounds better if the listener is on drugs, that's a can of worms I'm not prepared to open.

Electronic

Formed 1988.

Key Personnel: Bernard Sumner (vocals/guitar/keyboards), Johnny Marr (guitar).

There was a time when the term 'super group' sent a shudder down the spine as you knew it went hand in hand with the world's most self-indulgent music. Blind Faith, Emerson, Lake & Palmer, Cream. Each had an impressive ability to retreat up their own rectum.

Electronic, however, were a super group in every sense of the word. Bernard Sumner, singer and guitarist with the massively influential New Order, and Johnny Marr, guitarist with the legendary Smiths and widely recognised as one of the finest musicians of his generation - you don't get a lot more super than that. The original idea was for Marr to kick in a couple of tracks for a solo album Sumner was to make while New Order were on hiatus. Such were the pair's shared interests that it wasn't long before the solo project was scrapped and Electronic was brought into existence.

One of the first things the pair did was to hook up with another impressive duo, Neil Tennant and Chris Lowe, aka The Pet Shop Boys. It was a logical alliance given Tennant's admiration for the music of New Order (he lists 'Thieves Like Us' as his favourite ever song) and the fact that Sumner and Lowe had the same Italian dance records in their collections. That said, Sumner did express some discomfort about the situation: "It was a bit weird working with people as famous as Johnny and Neil: a bit oppressive." But when the end results were as beautiful as Electronic's debut single, 'Getting Away With It,' you could appreciate the benefit of having famous friends. Possessing the stamp of each of the contributing artists - Tennant's clipped Noel Coward-esque delivery, Marr's elegant guitar work, typically crap Sumner lyrics - the track made number 12 on the UK chart survey in December 1989.

Since The Pet Shop Boys and New Order were still very much going concerns, Electronic didn't record again for eighteen months (Marr killed time playing with Matt Johnson's The The) and when they did, Tennant would scale down his contribution to just two further tracks: the one-off single 'Disappointed'; and 'Patience Of A Saint,' one of the many stand-out features of Electronic's eponymous debut long-player. The summer album of 1991, it spawned two further singles, 'Feel Every Beat' and the divine 'Get The Message,' and contained so many fine tunes that the dismissive term 'project band' would never be attached to Electronic ever again.

Aside from the aforementioned 'Disappointed,' which made number 6 in July 1992, Electronic didn't release another record for four years, because Sumner fully rededicated himself to New Order. But when the critics struggled to find kind words to say about *Republic*, New Order's first LP for London Records, the singer retreated to the combined comforts of Electronic and Prozac. Sumner became involved with the latter as part of a BBC experiment to see how antidepressants affected artists and the creative process. In Sumner's case, the drugs were a bit of a double-edged sword as they elevated his mood but, in so doing, ate away the melancholia that informed so much of his songwriting. Electronic's second LP, *Forbidden City*, wasn't a bad record and singles like 'For You' and 'Second Nature' were an improvement on much of what charted in 1996. However, after the sublime quality of their first long-player, it was hard not to feel disappointed.

Electronic's third LP, *Twisted Tenderness*, was another perfunctory affair - the most remarkable thing about it was that it had a picture of Rasputin on the cover. But now that Sumner's back recording with New Order and Marr's busying himself with his new band, The Healers, and his fashion house, Elk, perhaps we can forget Electronic's more recent letdowns and instead savour the memory of their shiny, sensational contribution to the summer of 1991 and that fleeting moment when the term 'super group' ceased to be a dirty word.

Essential Song: 'Getting Away With It.' Sumptuous orchestration, gorgeous Spanish guitar and Bernard bleating on about how 'I've been walking in the rain just to get wet on purpose.' How did it fail to make the top 5?

Essential Album: *Electronic*. Ten great tracks, three chart singles, the number 2 position on the LP chart and, in 'Soviet,' one of the greatest instrumental tracks this side of Massive Attack. One of Madchester's true high points, it hasn't dated by a second.

Oasis

Formed 1993.

Key Personnel: Liam Gallagher (vocals), Noel Gallagher (vocals/guitar), Paul 'Bonehead' Arthurs (guitar), Paul 'Guigsy' McGuigan (bass), Alan White (drums).

They look like The Beatles, they sound like The Beatles and for a short while they were as big as The Beatles. But while they are deeply indebted to The Fab Four, Oasis owe just as much to their home town's magic hour - Madchester.

It was 1993 when 26-year-old Noel Gallagher approached his brother Liam's band Rain with a proposition. The deal was simple: the band had to give Noel complete creative control and in return he would make them rich beyond their wildest dreams. Since the group were no strangers to poverty (the Gallaghers had been raised by their mother on a biscuit factory worker's salary) they agreed to follow the ambitious masterplan.

Now called Oasis, the band rehearsed and toured hard. As other groups frantically played the music industry game, Gallagher Senior's courting of the labels extended to gate-crashing Glasgow's King Tut's Wah Wah Hut, where Creation Records bands 18 Wheeler and Boyfriend were gigging, and demanding that his band be allowed to play. Since Oasis had brought several beered-up friends along, the club owner had no choice but to let Oasis take the stage and so take away the breath of Creation boss Alan McGee, who was only at the gig because his sister had promised to bring along a friend he fancied.

The transition from freshly-signed group to the biggest band in the world wasn't quite the smooth ride it might have seemed. Indeed, Creation were so dissatisfied with the band's debut album *Definitely Maybe* that they hired producer Owen Morris to help the group re-record it. That the difficult days were behind Oasis became apparent the moment they unleashed their first single, 'Supersonic.' An awesome swaggering slab of rock 'n' roll, the song boasted possibly the greatest opening lines of any debut release: 'I've got to be myself/I can't be no one else.' That the record only reached number 33 was criminal. The group, however, showed a lack of concern which was borne out by the success of follow-up release 'Shakermaker' (a wholesale rip-off of The New Seekers' 'I'd Like To Teach The World To Sing' in some critics' eyes) which peaked at number 11.

The record that really turned things around for Oasis, however, was 'Live Forever.' Written by Noel as a riposte to the 'I hate myself and I want to die' angst of the grunge scene, its soaring optimism and delicious defiance powered it into the top ten. The epic if mildly tragic 'Cigarettes & Alcohol' followed the same path a few months later. And while Oasis were successfully conquering the singles chart, *Definitely Maybe* was racking up remarkable sales for a debut album. Few could argue that the record deserved to do so well. From the emphatic 'Rock 'N' Roll Star' to the sharp spite of 'Married With Children,' the album rarely misses a beat ('Digsy's Diner' was correctly identified by Al Spicer in *Rock: 100 Essential CDs* as *Definitely Maybe*'s "Ringo track") and frequently achieves greatness. And how did this critical and commercial success change the lives of the band members? As Bonehead explained to journalist Andrew Perry on the night the record went to the top of the charts: "I'm a number one recording artiste and all I've got is £1.40."

Bonehead's bank balance probably looked a bit better after the group wrapped up an astonishing 1994 with their first top-5 hit, 'Whatever.' The band's touring also swelled the coffers. As good as they were on record, it was as a live band that Oasis truly rocked. With well over a hundred gigs under their belt before the release of *Definitely Maybe*, the group went into overdrive now that they had a record to promote. And as the group got bigger and bigger, so the venues became truly colossal. Indeed, 1995 saw Oasis headline Glastonbury and play the biggest indoor gigs ever staged in Europe at Earl's Court. That the band had now become gigantic had everything to do with their second album, *(What's The Story) Morning Glory?* Six years later, the record seems a rather fat, conceited affair containing few truly great tracks and far too many references to other artists (while arch-rivals Blur suggested influences, Noel Gallagher would steal things wholesale, a practice that would lead to royalty demands from Stevie Wonder and The Bonzo Dog Doo Dah Band's Neil Innes). At the time, however, there didn't seem to be another record worth talking about. While Blur won the singles face-off between their 'Country House' and Oasis' (utterly dreadful) 'Roll With It,' *Morning Glory* devoured disappointing *Park Life* follow-up *The Great Escape*. And while Fran Healy might well ask: "What's a Wonderwall, anyway?" that single (which reached number 2 in November 1995), 'Some Might Say' (the group's first number one), 'Don't Look Back In Anger' (their second in March 1996) and 'Champagne Supernova' were all epic achievements. And what's more it wasn't just Britain that got the message about *Morning Glory*. The album made the top 5 in America and 'Wonderwall' broke into the Billboard top 10.

A multi-Platinum album, two number one singles, transatlantic triumph, four Brit awards and two concerts in front of 125,000 people at Knebworth - it was with some justice that Oasis could claim to be the biggest band in the world. As the success had come quickly so it had also come at a price: Guigsy suffered a nervous breakdown and had to skip a US tour; and original drummer Tony McCaroll was sacked because he couldn't play the new material and was replaced by Alan White. The hectic touring schedule and inflated egos also placed a strain on the Gallagher's rather fragile relationship (over the years, stories of one or the other of the boys leaving the band have become so common, they now fail to register).

It was after one such break-up rumour that the group set about recording their third album *Be Here Now*. Since they'd just made the fastest-selling album since Michael Jackson's *Bad* and had outsold the unit shifting machines that were Robson & Jerome and The Three Tenors (nicknamed "thirty quid" by the Gallagher boys), Creation were happy to let the band record the album however they pleased. They were considerably less chuffed when they heard the finished article. *Be Here Now*'s excesses were hinted at by its album cover art which included an homage to Keith Moon's Rolls-Royce/swimming pool interface. It was when the single 'D'You Know What I Mean' came out that it was apparent just how badly the band had gone awry. Sure, the track went to the top of the charts, but in the summer of 1997, Oasis were such a hot act they could have had number ones with nursery rhymes. Appallingly pompous, the song gave the world the rare opportunity to watch a band at the very moment that it disappeared up its own arse. Admittedly, later singles 'Stand By Me' and the very Beatles-esque 'All Around The World' were better but even they smacked of a band more interested in being musos rather than making great music.

Perhaps shaken by the critical failure of *Be Here Now* (while the album didn't sell anywhere near as well as *Morning Glory*, it still shifted more copies than most bands do in a lifetime), Noel Gallagher authorised the release of an Oasis B-sides album, *The Masterplan*, presumably to remind the world just how good a songwriter he could be. But while the album did leave people wondering why tracks like 'Acquiesce' (the closest rival to 'Live Forever' in the group's finest three-minute stakes), the title track and Royal Family theme song 'Half A World Away' hadn't been singles in their own right, *The Masterplan* also revealed the extent and the speed of Oasis' decline. Heard next to *Be Here Now*, the record also showed how bad a state the band's sound was in. Originally influenced in equal measure by The Beatles and The Stone Roses (one can imagine Noel in his bedroom raiding John Lennon's songbook while Liam was in his mimicking Ian Brown's moves), the group now simply seemed to be working their way through the A to Z of rock 'n' roll excess.

The group weren't happy campers anymore, either. Liam and Noel had been at one another's throats since birth but Bonehead and Guigsy had always seemed a pretty stable pair (the lukewarm water to the brothers' fire and ice). When both quit the band, many thought it spelt the end of Oasis. A shrewd businessman aware that only he and his brother were fundamentally important to the group, Noel Gallagher simply found two replacements, ex-Ride bassist Andy Bell and Heavy Stereo guitarist Gem, and had them re-record Bonehead's and McGuigan's contributions to the group's fourth LP proper. Gallagher Senior also hired the services of Mark 'Spike' Spitz on the grounds that the engineer/producer had an understanding of club culture. (Noel's own appreciation of dance music resulted in two collaborations with The Chemical Brothers, the first of which 'Setting Sun' went to number one in October 1996.) Not that *Standing On The Shoulder Of Giants* was a club-oriented album. It wasn't much of an album at all, really - just a couple of good tracks, 'Sunday Morning Call' and the Liam-penned 'Little James,' some appalling rhyming ('I see a liar/sitting by the fire') and a few Noel knock-offs (the chorus to number one single 'Go Let It Out' was lifted from a sixteenth-century poem, for fuck's sake). Indeed, the record was nowhere near as interesting as either Noel's decision to quit touring or Liam's bust-up with "fat dancer" Robbie

Williams. Live LP *Familiar To Millions*, released shortly afterwards, was equally underwhelming.

It's debatable whether *Standing On The Shoulder Of Giants* was an improvement on *Be Here Now* but there can be no argument that the record failed to recapture the glory of, er, *Morning Glory*. To say that a group as big of Oasis is at crisis point sounds perverse. Even someone as cocksure as Noel Gallagher must have some concerns for the future. Music fans should be worried, too. They might not be your favourite group but Oasis did more than any other band to make British music an entity people cared about and something the world heard about. They were also instrumental in the success of the very worthy *Help* LP (the band brilliantly re-recorded ace B-side 'Fade Away' and Noel collaborated with Paul Weller and Sir Paul McCartney on a cover of 'Come Together'), contributed a standout track to the Jam tribute LP *Fire & Skill* (a version of 'Carnation' recorded with Ocean Colour Scene's Steve Craddock and that man Weller again) and were responsible for some of the finest concerts of the late twentieth century. And as for preserving the Madchester sound beyond its 1992 use-by date, the group deserve a reward for services to conservation.

Of course, they can also be pretty embarrassing. The brothers' showbiz marriages and divorces meant the group spent too much time in *Hello!* magazine and not enough in *Q*. Noel and Liam's constant bickering is also a little tiresome. However, as they acknowledged in 'Acquiesce,' the Gallaghers need one another. And does the world still need Oasis? Definitely. Maybe.

Essential Song: 'Live Forever.' Oasis fans recently voted this the band's greatest single and who am I to disagree? Quite simply, a record about being glad to be alive that makes you feel the same way.

Essential Album: *Definitely Maybe*. Right up there with *The Stone Roses* and *The Smiths* on the list of great album debuts. It's been downhill ever since but when you scale Everest on your first attempt, where else is there to go?

6. Lost In Music

Just as in the 1970s, for every Joy Division there were a thousand bands that didn't make it, so at the height of the baggy boom, there were countless flop acts for every Happy Mondays. Foremost amongst Madchester's failures were Northside, a perfectly reasonable band who had the misfortune to become the preferred act of DJ-cum-twat Jonathan King. Incredibly well hyped, the group never really recovered from such a dubious endorsement and after three unsuccessful attempts to crack the top 40, they went their separate ways.

Marginally more successful were The Mock Turtles. Lead by Martin Coogan, brother of comedy actor Steve, the group had the good sense to record one astonishingly excellent single, 'Can You Dig It?' Sadly, Coogan saw this as an excuse to become insufferably conceited. Examples of his arrogance included comparing himself to Ikea furniture in an interview with *Record Mirror* ("I'm well built and stylish") and, at a gig at Birmingham University, taking off his shoes and socks and then thrusting his feet into the crowd so that his audience could 'enjoy' them. So busy was Coogan at making a prat of himself that he completely forgot to write any more astonishingly excellent singles and The Mock Turtles were soon no more. You could say they had a short shell life.

Flowered Up were a London-based act whose Madchester credentials became apparent the moment they appeared in the *NME* even before they had released a single. Despite such impressive props, the group's first four singles failed to do anything and we would not be talking about them at all were it not for 'Weekender,' a breathtaking, hazy ode to 48 hour party people complete with a 28-minute-long video directed by the innovative and appropriately named Wiz which starred Lee Whitlock, most recently seen in the movie *Hard Men*. It wasn't sufficient to sustain a career but the fact the promo still airs on late night MTV proves that Flowered Up weren't just another pop novelty.

Which is perhaps more than can be said for The High, about whom the only remarkable things were that they featured one time Stone Rose Andy Couzens and that when they realised they weren't going to make it as a baggy outfit, their lead singer John Matthews devoured a whole sheet of acid and washed it down with a bottle of brandy. When, a year later, The High re-emerged as a grunge band, it was noted that Matthews looked as if 'he had just got back from Vietnam.'

While The High only managed to crack the top 40 on one occasion, Ireland's The Frank & Walters made it all the way to number 11 with the Roses-esque 'After All.' A perfectly serviceable track, remixed by The Lightning Seeds' Ian Broudie, there was, nevertheless, a rather forced feel about the enterprise. It had a sense of inauthenticity which became more evident when the band appeared on *Top Of The Pops* looking about as comfortable in their baggy gear as Bernard Manning in a tutu. Whether they meant it or not, one flop single later and it was back to the bogs for The Frank & Walters.

Of course, all success is relative, and since a part of the Madchester ethos was that there was nothing left to lose, you could argue that in simply forming a band, securing a record deal, releasing a single and/or enjoying chart success, all of the above acts were winners. They just didn't win very big.

7. Bog Awful Baggy

And while many bands didn't get it right, several more simply didn't get it.

As with anything fashionable, Madchester spawned its share of imitators. The most successful of these was EMF. Hailing from that musical hotbed The Forest Of Dean, they wore the right clothes (they were particularly big on Vision Street Wear), had an appropriate sound (they invested a lot of faith in synths and heavy bass) and possessed a Mondays-esque eye for controversy (their name stood for, get the children in mother, Ecstasy Mother Fuckers). What they didn't have was more than one decent song. Their decent song, 'Unbelievable,' was so original it reached the number one spot in America and went top three in the UK. And from those giddy heights, the band rapidly tumbled. A follow-up single, 'I Believe,' was basically a reworking of their breakthrough single. Their debut album *Schubert Dip* (the title was inspired by songwriter Derry Brownson's tendency to raid the classics when he ran out of ideas) sold well enough to finance a second, *Stigma*, which sold badly but nowhere near as badly as LP number 3, *Cha Cha Cha*. By this time, the group were so desperate to shift units they i) were willing to provide support for Vic Reeves on his shocking cover of The Monkees' 'I'm A Believer' and ii) happy to stick the three best-known tracks from *Schubert Dip* on the CD single for 'Afro King.' And that was where EMF's career should have ended. Dropped by their label in 1997, they were each off doing their own thing when, completely out of the blue, they were offered a chance to play a reunion concert in Italy. One gig later and the group were making plans to tour the world. Don't be surprised if you find them playing a residency next time you visit Hemsby Pontins.

Marginally less annoying (and we really are only talking marginally) were Liverpool's The Farm. Originally a ska band, the group jumped the Madchester gravy train with, of all things, 'Groovy Train,' an upbeat, unambitious three-and-a-half-minuter which made the top 10 in September 1990. A follow-up, the anthemic 'Altogether Now' did even better and heralded a brief alliance with Pete Wylie, formerly of The Mighty Wah! To put the icing on the cake, The Farm's *Spartacus* album, complete with its innovative soap box design cover, went platinum. A second album, the racially aware but musically moribund *Love See No Colour*, did nowhere near as well and the three singles released from it all stiffed. It was some indication of the band's shortage of ideas and lack of musical ambition that the only time they'd again trouble the top 30 would be with a work-manlike cover of The Human League's 'Don't You Want Me?' But then again, The Farm always did feel a bit like chancers. At least they had the apparent honesty to admit they'd been lucky to get where they did. For the video for 'Don't You Want Me?,' they surrendered all ambitions to high art and/or slickness and instead used it as a chance to meet their hero, soc-cer legend George Best.

While it didn't take long for The Farm's bubble to burst, it took an absolute age for Jesus Jones' balloon to inflate. When the band's first three singles each stalled on the outskirts of the top 40, it must have looked like they were never going to make it. Although they didn't exactly sound like a Manc band (they had a pretty nondescript synth and guitar led brand of Indie pop), the group pushed the baggy look and eventually cracked the top 20 with 'Real Real Real' in April 1990. When their next release, the actually rather good 'Right Here Right Now,' failed to repeat this success, Jesus Jones simply redonned the baseball caps, shot a swirly Stone Roses-style video and, hey presto, they were sitting at number 7 with 'International Bright Young Thing.' A more ironic title it's hard to think of, for after 'Right Here Right Now' bombed for a second time and 'The Devil You Know' briefly grazed the top 10, they were back to the disappointing chart positions of their early career. Baseball caps off to them for keeping it up until 1997, mind.

A brief career as a pretend baggy band didn't necessarily mean a brief career in pop music, however. Take Seymour. When the Colchester-based band signed with Food Records, their contract stipulated that they must change their name, which they did to Blur, and pursue a particular musical style. The upshot of this was *Leisure*, an undistinguished album that com-bined fine songs, principally 'There's No Other Way' and 'Sing,' with a willingness to exploit the prevailing fashion of the day. In their quest to align themselves with Madchester, the group sported long, sculpted mul-lets and wore big, tie-dye shirts of the sort Ian Brown was often seen in. The short-term gains of this policy were quite impressive - 'There's No Other Way' reached number 8 in the spring of 1991. As Damon Albarn has since come to admit, the fact that Blur's next single, the atrocious 'Bang' ("Our worst ever song," the singer now claims), failed to chart highly was no bad thing. With the gimmick being seen to have failed, the band were now free to make the sort of sound they wanted. The immediate fruits of this were the truly stunning 'Pop Scene,' one of the finest singles of the decade, and *Modern Life Is Rubbish*, one of the greatest British LPs of all time. And if you don't agree with these lofty claims, well you can write your own book!

Like American soldiers in Vietnam, Blur's misguided flirtation with baggy wasn't their fault. They were just following orders. The actions of Scotland's The Soup Dragons, on the other hand, seemed far more calculating. Going nowhere fast with their brand of 'spiky pop freneticism,' as James Sutherland describes it in *The Rough Guide To Rock*, the group seemingly swapped influences overnight. The Buzzcocks and The Stooges instantaneously gave way to the Mondays and The Stone Roses. When The Soup Dragons (they took their name from children's TV favourite *The Clangers*) trooped onto *Top Of The Pops* to perform their loved-up cover of The Rolling Stones' 'I'm Free' with Black Uhuru's Junior Reid, it was like watching a bunch of Roses impersonators on *Stars In Their Eyes*. Not that the similarity hurt their records sales ('I'm Free' made the top 10). But while you can't blame a struggling band for buying into baggy, The Soup Dragons' bandwagon jumping didn't fool anyone. Even the kids saw through it, as became apparent at the Smash Hits Poll Winners Party when 'Mother Universe' was voted the worst single of 1990. With the game up, the group tried to change their spots again but a brief flirtation with guitar pop was just that. Come 1992, they were back on the dole.

Although The Soup Dragons sold their soul, if there is a seventh level of imitation Madchester hell, you can bet that Candy Flip are living in it. Do you like 'Strawberry Fields Forever'? Yeah, everybody likes 'Strawberry Fields Forever.' But wouldn't you like it better if it was 'sung' over a synthetic symbol and snare drum by a man who appeared to be more primate than person? No, of course, you bloody wouldn't! That this very recipe was sufficient to secure a top-5 (top-5!) chart position in 1990 suggested that the kids really were taking too many drugs, or that Madchester had reached that point of popularity where even the most messed-up project had some chance of unit shifting success. Fortunately, a second single, 'This Can Be Real,' had the decency to flop dreadfully and Candy Flip disappeared in the direction of the nearest who-cares-where-they-are-now file.

8. Rave On?

Just as people have tried to pinpoint the death of the American West, critics have scrambled to tag the end of the Madchester scene to a specific moment in time. Precisely which event suggested that the party was over is a moot point. The more pessimistic pundits say the movement's death throes began as early as The Stone Roses' disastrous Spike Island concert (exactly whose bright idea was it to stage an event in the middle of nowhere, using a stage set-up that left the audiences so far from the act, they might as well have been attending a Space Shuttle launch and a PA that would have shamed a Rotherham working men's club?). Others claim the band's many years in the making follow-up LP *Second Coming* had a definite nail-in-the-coffin quality about it. But whether it was either of these atrocities or New Order's prolonged hiatus or the Mondays' over-stimulated, under-rehearsed ... *Yes Please* that indicated Madchester's time was up, by the time The Roses played the 1996 Reading Festival with a line-up featuring just two members of the original line-up, there was no question that the North was no longer at its heights.

But if the scene proper was dead, it continued to exist as a national music-shaping force. Indeed, in the mid-90s there was even talk of a second Madchester explosion, as acts like Oasis, Intastella/World Of Twist and Black Grape recaptured some of the excitement of five years earlier. It's also worth remembering how many baggy bands are still with us. Besides the massively successful James, The Charlatans, New Order, Ian Brown, 808 State and A Guy Called Gerald remain fixtures at the major European dance festivals and, even as I write, former Inspiral Carpets frontman Tim Hingley is probably belting out 'This Is How It Feels' in your local dive.

But it's not just the bands that have endured - it's the sound. Indeed, you can take virtually any important British act post-Madchester and trace their musical heritage back to baggy. Brit Pop? Well, while it did have a lot to do with Madness, Slade, The Kinks and The Small Faces, Noel Gallager has gone on record as saying: "No Roses, No Oasis." Likewise, the UK dance boom, although undeniably shaped by Ibiza and New York, wouldn't exist without the North-West's club culture as, arguably, might not the country's huge appetite for Ecstasy. And as for Superstar DJs - without the Hacienda, you'd still think a disc jockey was a guy who played weddings and liked to 'stick on something slow for the ladies.' So whether you loved it or loathed it, it doesn't matter - if you don't own records shaped by the Madchester sound, well then you haven't got a record collection.

If you still need tangible evidence that interest in Madchester persists, look no further than...

24 Hour Party People (2001)

Cast: Steve Coogan (Tony Wilson), Paddy Considine (Rob Gretton), Danny Cunningham (Shaun Ryder), Sean Harris (Ian Curtis), Shirley Henderson (Lindsey Wilson), Lennie James (Alan Erasmus), Peter Kay (Don Tonay), Ralf Little (Peter Hook), Andy Serkis (Martin Hannett), John Simm (Bernard Sumner), Raymond Waring (Vini Reilly).

Crew: Director Michael Winterbottom, Producer Andrew Eaton, Writer Frank Cottrell Boyce, Cinematographer Robby Muller, Editor Trevor Waite, Art Directors David Bryan & Paul Cripps, Costume Design Natalie Ward.

Story: The complete history of Factory Records, from Tony Wilson and Alan Erasmus founding the label and the infamous Hacienda to the formation of Joy Division, the death of Ian Curtis, the birth of New Order and the rise and demise of the Happy Mondays.

Origins: There had been talk of a Madchester movie from the moment someone realised there was a scene. As early as 1990, Factory were talking about filming the Happy Mondays story. Provisionally entitled *The Mad Fackers*, John Altman (*EastEnders*' Nick Cotton) was tipped to star, but the project never made it to the pre-production stage. There has also been speculation that a film might be based on *Touching From A Distance*, the memoirs of Ian Curtis' wife Deborah.

As for *24 Hour Party People*, it originally looked as if Danny Boyle (*Shallow Grave, Trainspotting, A Life Less Ordinary*) would take on the project in an effort to get over the financial and critical failure of *The Beach*. A good choice given his interest in youth culture and his Mancunian ancestry, Boyle eventually wound up shooting the non-Madchester related dramas *Vacuuming Completely Nude In Paradise* and *Strumpet* for the BBC. He is now working on a picture scripted by *The Beach* author Alex Garland.

Boyle's replacement, Michael Winterbottom, was an interesting choice if only because of his wildly eclectic CV. A Lancastrian, his work ranges from the first episode of *Cracker* to *Butterfly Kiss* (a North-West spree killer drama starring *Pulp Fiction*'s Angela Plummer), the Roddy Doyle-scripted TV series *Family*, an adaptation of Thomas Hardy's *Jude* starring Kate Winslet, the critically acclaimed *Welcome To Sarajevo* (based on the Balkan experiences of ITV newsman Michael Nicholson) and the excellent, experimental *Wonderland*, whose ensemble cast featured Gina McKee, Ian Hart and John Simm. His last work prior to *24 Hour Party People* was *The Claim*, a dark, driven drama about life in a North American mining community starring Peter Mullan (*My Name Is Joe*, *Braveheart*) and written by Frank Cottrell Boyce with whom Winterbottom would collaborate on this movie.

Even if *24 Hour Party People* had nothing else going for it, you'd have to congratulate Wendy Brazington on a terrific casting job. Besides the sensitive Simm being a first-class choice for New Order's frontman, you can think of few people better qualified to play the swaggering, up-to-no-good Peter Hook than *The Royle Family*'s Ralf Little. It's also impressive that she resisted the temptation to assign major stars to showy roles as Shaun Ryder and Ian Curtis, instead casting actors who were right for the parts. It's nice too, to see Peter Kay, one of Channel 4's finest discoveries, getting a stab at big-screen acting. And as for Steve Coogan as Tony Wilson, you only have to imagine a slick Alan Partridge to appreciate that he's perfect for the part.

There are some cracking cameos, too. Hacienda DJ and M People founder Mike Pickering spins discs in a recreation of the fabled club so accurate, it's hard to believe they ever knocked the place down. Mark E Smith gets a chance to again hurl abuse at Tony Wilson. Simon Pegg, star and co-author of the excellent *Spaced*, plays a journalist who gatecrashes Ian Curtis' funeral. And ex-Buzzcock Howard Devoto appears as a toilet cleaner. All this plus Paul Ryder playing himself, Mock Turtle Martin Coogan, Stone Rose Mani, Kenny Baker (R2D2 from the *Star Wars* trilogy), Rob Brydon (*Marion & Geoff*) and James Cartwright, son of playwright Jim (*The Rise & Fall Of Little Voice*), playing Steven Patrick Morrissey.

Off-Screen: The making of *24 Hour Party People* was a relatively straightforward affair. It was after shooting that problems emerged, first during a press conference at which Tony Wilson got upset when a reporter questioned his theory that there is a music revolution every 13 years and then later when the cast attended the Cannes Film Festival on a promotional tour. The cause of this second bout of controversy was actor Danny

Cunningham who had taken his being cast as Shaun Ryder to extremes, brawling with journalists and throwing around what appeared to be the bodies of dead pigeons. Suitably appalled, the clientele of the exclusive Majestic Hotel complained and Cunningham and Co. were ejected from the premises. Cunningham, who received a cut to the head during the mêlée, told the press that: "I think Shaun would have been proud of us. We came to Cannes to be wild and now we are going home." The pigeons, incidentally, were stage props that had been stuffed with fake blood. Their stunt, meanwhile, was in memory of an incident from Ryder's dark past in which he's said to have poisoned 3,000 of Manchester's finest flying rats with crack cocaine. (Although as any schoolboy could have told him, for the best results, you should feed birds Alka Seltzer because their stomachs cannot tolerate the effervescence and they explode. Please, for the love of God, don't try this at home.)

Rave On: Michael Winterbottom: "(Producer) Andrew Eaton and I were in British Columbia about 500 miles North of Vancouver in a Country and Western bar and we decided it would be a good idea to make a movie about that music, so after about thirty seconds we decided that Factory was the obvious story and Tony Wilson should be the main character. We talked to (screenwriter) Frank Cottrell Boyce about it. I met up with Steve Coogan and tried to persuade him and it gradually came from that. Of course, I foolishly thought that Factory would have some money...

"Part of the original idea was that the script would be quite loose. In a way, part of the attraction of making a film about Factory is that when you read about it, it sounds fairly shambolic. The idea of Factory was not to plan things too much, not to work like a company but to work as a group of people who let other people do what they wanted to do. So the idea was that the film would have the same spirit, that anyone who was working on it would be as free as possible to do what they wanted to do. The whole thing's kind of a shambles, but hopefully in the same way Factory was.

"It's really difficult when you're talking about making a movie about real people. At the same time, we weren't trying to make a documentary. We were lucky in that most of the people we talked to felt relaxed enough about it. It's great to have Paul Ryder acting in the movie and lots of people came down and did bits and pieces."

Steve Coogan: "Michael rang me up and said he was doing a movie about the Manchester music scene and he wanted me to play Tony Wilson. Lots of reasons endeared me to it. I'd worked with Tony about 10 years ago on a local television programme so I knew him from that. Also, I'd grown up with him on television and I was aware of Factory and I bought Joy Division records and I used to go to the Hacienda. The subject matter was close to my heart and I felt very proprietorial about it. It was not necessarily that I wanted to play Tony but that I didn't want anyone else to play Tony Wilson. I felt that I could do it better than anyone else.

"If Dave Wannabe Director had come up to me and said he wanted to do a film about Manchester, I would have been very, very worried but the combination of the subject matter and Michael and Andrew's reputation made it worthwhile.

"Certain parts of the story were invented for dramatic purposes. But other parts are exactly as they happened. It's a mishmash. I was talking to Tony and he said: 'If you ask anyone about this period, they'll have their own take on it and everyone's version of it will be slightly different.' They're all true.

"There's no cheesy lines like: 'Let's make our own rock 'n' roll! Let's build our own club!' It's brutally raw in some places. I don't think this film makes anybody look that cool."

Mani: "I thought the guy playing Bez looked brilliant. The guys playing the Mondays were nice kids as well. It's strange watching somebody else taking off your friends, weird! But it would probably have been even more strange watching someone taking off me, very odd."

The Verdict: As you might have gathered from this book, everyone has their own take on the Madchester scene. While fans of the movement listened to the same music and adored the same bands, their interpretations of both the sounds and the significance of Madchester vary immensely. This personal angle ought to pose huge problems for a film like *24 Hour Party People* or, at least, it would if the movie set out to deliver a 'definitive' account. It is to Michael Winterbottom's credit that he offers up a version of events rather than the final word on the matter. These events are, of course, quite remarkable but fortunately Winterbottom's direction and Frank Boyce's tight script are too. And as for the performances, Steve Coogan couldn't be more like Tony Wilson if he altered his DNA, Ralf Little, John Simm and Lennie James all punch well above their weight, and Danny Cunnigham and Sean Harris couldn't do a finer job of essaying the movement's most charismatic characters. But even with everyone firing on all cylinders, the movie could still have cocked everything up if it had forgotten to include the great sounds and massive doses of sarcasm that were so much a part of the scene. So funky that it will make you believe the Hacienda never closed its doors, and so funny it shames most of what passes for British comedy, *24 Hour Party People* couldn't be more Madchester if it sported a 'Cool As Fuck' T-shirt. To put it another way, you'd be a mad facker not to catch it. 4/ 5

"Madchester - one of those terms that'll be around forever."

- Bez, Happy Mondays

9. Reference Materials

As you can imagine, a complete list of reference works would run the length of this book. What you'll find below is simply the best of the best.

Books

Touching From A Distance by Deborah Curtis and Jon Savage, Faber & Faber, GB, 2001, Paperback, 212 pages, £8.99, ISBN: 0571207391. A book one doubts Tony Wilson keeps on his bedside table. Not only does *Touching From A Distance* paint the Factory boss in a none-too-favourable light, it also shatters a few myths about legendary lost boy Curtis. Co-written by Jon Savage (a huge fan of Joy Division and New Order and the author of such revered works as *England's Dreaming* and *The Faber Book Of Pop*), this memoir is shot through with a beguiling mix of stark, understandable bitterness and truly ennobling sincerity. A beautiful book about a brittle, much missed Englishman.

Hallelujah! The Extraordinary Return Of Shaun Ryder & The Happy Mondays by Shaun Ryder and John Warburton, Virgin Publishing, GB, 2000, Paperback, 221 pages, £12.99, ISBN: 0753504235. It's a pity Ryder didn't write his memoirs when he was at the height of his creative powers. Still, there's very little here that's dull and quite a lot that's amusing, mind-boggling, disgusting and weirdly wise.

Freaky Dancin': Me And The Mondays by Bez, Pan, GB, 2000, Paperback, 340 pages, £6.99, ISBN: 0330481975. An entertaining book written by a man who's obviously far more intelligent than he's ever let on. This not only compliments Ryder's book but also serves as a tribute to the human mind and its ability to recall events even when one is completely monkeyed.

Shaun Ryder: Happy Mondays, Black Grape & Other Traumas by Mick Middles, Independent Music Press, GB, 1997, Paperback, 202 pages, £9.99, ISBN: 1897783116. Arguably the best book written about Madchester's clown prince, if only because it was penned before his recent descent into pantomime and crippling drug abuse. And if you're still curious to find out exactly what's going on in Shaun's addled mind, you could do worse than track down Middles' *Shaun Ryder: In His Own Words*, also published by Independent Music Press.

Take Me There: Oasis The Story by Paul Mathur, Bloomsbury Press, GB, 1997, 288 pages, £5.99, ISBN: 0747533881. There are far too many books about Oasis on the market. Mathur's scores over the others because he respects the band but, although the book includes an introduction by the Brothers Gallagher, he doesn't fully buy into the idea that they were the saviours of modern music. A detailed, sober study of a far from sober band.

The Charlatans - The Authorised History by Dominic Willis, Virgin Publishing, GB, 2000, 219 pages, £12.99, ISBN: 0753504774. With a foreword written by Tim Burgess, *Uncut* magazine said this was 'as close to definitive as you get,' and it's hard to disagree.

The Stone Roses And The Resurrection Of British Pop by John Robb, Ebury Press, GB, 1997, 395 pages, £7.99, ISBN: 009187887X. Robb has a laugh like a hyena and looks like an ageing Vanilla Ice, but you shouldn't let that put you off since this is pretty much essential reading. You should also try and get hold of Robb's *The '90s - What The Fuck Was That All About?,* also published by Ebury.

The Complete Guide To The Music Of The Smiths by Johnny Rogan, Omnibus Press, GB, 1995, 126 pages, £5.99, ISBN: 071194900X. Pretty much all you could need to know about the music of this truly indispensable band. And what's more it's CD shaped so it'll fit nicely in between your copies of *Meat Is Murder* and *The Queen Is Dead.*

Morrissey & Marr: The Severed Alliance by Johnny Rogan, Omnibus Press, GB, 1993, 360 pages, £12.95, ISBN: 0711930007. Quite simply, one of the most important books about British music ever written. Rather like Patrick Humphries' biography of Nick Drake, Nick Tosches' *Dino* and *Dear Boy,* Tony Fletcher's book about Keith Moon, anyone who considers themselves a music lover should own this book.

Primal Scream by Stuart Coles, Omnibus Press, GB, 1998, 64 pages, £8.99, ISBN: 0711968071. Not great but it'll do until somebody subjects the group to in-depth study.

The following are currently out of print but you might be able to track them down in second-hand stores or specialist shops such as the superb Helter Skelter in London's Denmark Street.

New Order & Joy Division - Pleasures & Wayward Distractions by Brian Edge. A book I'm hugely fond of as it assisted my introduction to these two bands. Admiring without being reverent, detailed without being obsessive, funny without being frivolous - it's a travesty that this book isn't around to accompany New Order's glorious return.

The Charlatans - We Are Rock by John Robb. This is a wonderful study written by a man who clearly respects the band's desire to stay together as much as their music. From the same series that brought us Angus Batey's awesome *Rhyming & Stealing - A History Of The Beastie Boys*.

Breaking Into Heaven: The Rise & Fall Of The Stone Roses by Mick Middles. That man Middles again with a book that can't compete with Robb's epic tome but which doesn't really try to. Entertaining and informative, this is another impressive work from a biographer who's also written essential tomes on comedian Frankie Howerd and Echo & The Bunnymen's lead singer Ian McCulloch.

Videos

The Happy Mondays Party At G-MEX 25.3.90 (WIV001)
New Order - Academy (deleted)
Neworderstory (deleted)
Oasis - Familiar To Millions (RKIDVHS005)
The Smiths - The Complete Picture (4509911553)
The Complete Stone Roses (WNR2057)
The Stone Roses - Blackpool Live (WIV006)

DVDs

New Order - Live (8573848022)
Oasis - Live By The Sea (RKIDDVD022)
Oasis - Familiar To Millions (RKIDDVD005)
Oasis - Then & There (2015139)
The Smiths - The Complete Picture (4509911552)

Websites

The information superhighway is littered with Madchester-centric sites many of which are of piss-poor quality and/or rarely updated. What follows is simply a list of six of the best scene-related stop-off points.

New Order Official US Website - www.neworderweb.com - How appropriate that one of the world's finest bands should have one of the Web's greatest sites. As flawless as much of the group's music.

Ian Brown Official Site - www.ianbrown-online.co.uk - The ex-Stone Roses frontman's site not only contains a wealth of information but also exposes King Monkey's very healthy sense of humour. I mean, if you'd been teased your whole life about your simian features, would you set up a site containing details about how to help save the orang-utan?

I Am Without Shoes - www.stoneroses.net - There are actually plenty of good Stone Roses sites around. This, however, scores extra points on account of it being so idiosyncratic. The American fans' pseudo-religious essays are a particular delight.

The Charlatans - www.thecharlatans.net - A band that continues to excite and surprise offers up a superb official website.

Primal Scream - www.repriserec.com/primalscream/ - Another excellent band-endorsed effort. This is worth checking out for the downloads alone.

Cemetry Gates - www.moz.pair.com - Smiths sites are as common on the web as pornography (so I'm told). This being so, Cemetry Gates (sic) might not be the best but it appears to be amongst the most comprehensive.